the teaching game

DR DAMIEN BARRY

the teaching game

A HANDBOOK FOR SURVIVING AND THRIVING IN THE CLASSROOM

This book is dedicated to my Year 12 English class of 2022, for you helped me to find what I thought I had lost. You each gave me more than I could ever give you!

Published in 2023 by Amba Press, Melbourne, Australia
www.ambapress.com.au

© Damien Barry 2023

All rights reserved. No part of this book may be reproduced or transmitted in any form or by any means, electronic or mechanical, including photocopying, recording or by any information storage and retrieval system, without prior permission in writing from the publisher.

Cover design: Tess McCabe
Internal design: Amba Press
Editor: Francesca Hoban-Ryan
Printing: IngramSpark

ISBN: 9781922607683 (pbk)
ISBN: 9781922607690 (ebk)

A catalogue record for this book is available from the National Library of Australia.

Contents

Introduction		1
Part A: the science of teaching		**5**
1	The twin Rs: relationships and rapport	7
2	Planning and the five Ps	13
3	Theories, models and frameworks: making sense of the education jungle	29
4	Methods of instruction: what to use and when to use it	37
5	Using data to inform practice	47
Part B: the art of teaching		**57**
6	What is this thing called pedagogy?	59
7	Assessment tasks, criteria and rubrics	63
8	Teaching kids on the spectrum	75
9	Boys and girls: do they learn differently, and if they do then so what?	87
10	Feedback: how and when to give it	95
Part C: the practicalities of teaching		**101**
11	Classroom management 101	103
12	Teacher performance and development	109
13	Differentiation: how does it work?	115

14	Future skills: what else do we need to teach and how do we do it?	119
15	Collegiality: we all need a teacher buddy	125
16	A brief blurb about AITSL and the Australian Professional Standards for Teachers	131
17	Getting yourself classroom-fit	135

Conclusion   141

References   143

Acknowledgements   147

About the author   149

Introduction

This is the book I wish I'd had when I began my undergraduate teaching degree as a keen but clueless 18-year-old on the first steps of what would become a lifelong career. It's the book I wish I'd had when I was doing assignments on the theories that underpin teaching and learning. It's the book I wish I'd had when I was trying to wrap my head around classroom management, unit planning, assessment tasks, marking criteria and some strange phenomenon called an 'anticipatory set'. (I later found out this was just a fancy name for grabbing the attention of the class at the start of a lesson. Why not call it an 'attention-grabber' instead of leaving us first-year students scratching our heads for the next three months!)

As is the case with undergraduates, I was doing all these things before I ever stepped into a classroom with my teacher hat on. To learn about the fundamentals of teaching was a whole new world of theorists, models, frameworks, learning styles, principles, structures, scaffolds and formats. And that was before we even started to look at lesson content and how to engage a large group of disparate teenagers with only a cursory interest in the subject.

This is the book I wish I'd had when I was trying to put into practice everything I had learned at university, and quickly realising that much of it didn't have a real-world application in the classroom. Or when I had about 100 hours' worth of content to fit into 50 hours of lesson time. Or when the 10-week stretch of term ahead forced me to figure out that I needed to write the assessment task first, then cover content that would enable my students to do reasonably well, then spread this out logically week-to-week. Later I discovered that this process was called backward mapping or backwards by design. No one taught me the practical approaches to planning and teaching that allow an early-career teacher to survive.

This is the book I wish I'd had when I began mentoring and coaching teachers across all phases of their careers. When as Head of Department, Head of Middle School, Deputy Headmaster or Principal I was charged with supporting other teachers who—like me—were trying their best to juggle the demands of teaching. When I was doing lesson observations, trying to get a class of rowdy kids to behave, helping plan a decent unit and showing colleagues what differentiation looked like. When I was instructing a group of early-career teachers on how to set up their classrooms to give themselves a fighting chance of success in Term 1. When I was providing suggestions to these same teachers about how to get and stay classroom-fit so they could remain upright and breathing with some semblance of sanity by December.

If only I'd had a guide that would make a positive difference to the lessons I prepared, the students I taught, the assessment I wrote, the feedback I provided, the colleagues with whom I shared a staffroom. If only I'd had a guide to increasing my fulfilment and job satisfaction.

It has become apparent to me that many teachers, regardless of experience, have at best a basic understanding of good teaching. The profession tends to overcomplicate the craft. One only needs to go to a university library and look at the rows of shelves containing a huge number of books dissecting theories. The typical undergraduate course takes 4 years to complete. That's roughly 32 subjects and 64 assignments created to pump content into the head of a trainee teacher who is then sent into the jungle of a school; the same jungle that so many teachers leave after five years of struggle. Like you, these teachers started their university journey full of hope and made it through determined to make a difference to the lives of young people.

Many teachers are still unsure of the fundamentals of our profession: how to interpret an assessment rubric, why it's important to build rapport with your students, how to write a decent assessment task, how to help students who need both support and extension, how to provide effective feedback and how to manage disruptive behaviour. Although this stuff is ostensibly taught at university and during school practicums, I see gaps and weaknesses every day. Teachers have a moral and ethical obligation to understand these fundamentals. Teaching is so much more than just knowing your content: it's about bringing it to life in the mind of a student.

I love teaching. It is a brilliant career that provides so much joy and fulfilment. But teaching is also hard. It can be a messy and emotionally draining job. I aim to help teachers to avoid burnout and thrive in the classroom.

I started my career in the mid-1990s and remain in the classroom to this day. Although I'm now a principal, the classroom remains my happy place. It gives me sanctuary and comfort, and it keeps me energised. I still make plenty of mistakes and leave a lesson kicking myself if I know I did a poor job. I still plan units of work, and try to write assessment that is relevant and interesting. I still provide plenty of scribbled pencil feedback on drafts. I still have difficulties managing a classroom of teenagers, trying to get them settled enough to learn about essay writing when they just had their own version of a State of Origin rugby league game on the oval during break. Although I have good and bad lessons, I have learned enough across three decades, several schools and assorted states and countries to know what works.

This book is called *The Teaching Game* for a reason. Teachers need to have a game plan and a few tactics in order to win, and we need a way to measure our success. We have both opponents and teammates. To help us we have equipment, tools and resources. There are external elements that will affect our play and influence the outcome.

Our playing field is the classroom. It may not be polite to call students our opponents, but I'm sure you get the picture! Our game plan is the lesson plan. Our tactics are how we deliver content and manage behaviour. Our equipment includes our voice, energy, whiteboard and laptop. Our teammates are our colleagues. The external elements are parents, the curriculum and a timetable that may bless you with the last lesson on a Friday with a Year 8 class. The outcome is the assessment result, the end-of-semester report or even just seeing a kid be happy. We are in a game, so let's play it well enough that we can win the damn thing!

For ease of understanding and consumption, this book is split into three parts:

- **Part A:** The Science of Teaching
- **Part B:** The Art of Teaching
- **Part C:** The Practicalities of Teaching

The Science of Teaching covers core aspects that are theoretical or grounded in research. The Art of Teaching covers the stuff that brings content to life and joy to a classroom. The Practicalities of Teaching covers everything they don't teach you at university: how to create a decent lesson, engage kids, reduce disruption and keep your own energy up for as long as it takes.

Welcome to the teaching game. You have chosen wisely. Now buckle up and hold on tight!

PART A

the science of teaching

1
The twin Rs: relationships and rapport

We deliver content, but we teach children. I cannot stress enough the importance of building a positive connection with your students. Children listen to a teacher who genuinely enjoys their company and wants to get to know them on a deeper level. Developing a positive relationship makes it much easier to get and maintain the attention of your students. They will learn more effectively and accept your verbal and written feedback more readily. You can then begin to experiment in class with different strategies and activities. You can trade on this relationship and rapport because your students will see that you are trying something designed to benefit them and want to see it work. All of this adds to the joy of teaching and learning.

The relationship that you establish with your students often transfers to their parents. Many children go home and talk about their day. Positive discussions strengthen the partnership between home and school. You will see the results of this at parent-teacher interviews and in academic reporting.

Now here's the disclaimer: the establishment of rapport is not about being a best friend to your students. It's not about agreeing with every bright idea they have, and it's not about avoiding conflict or pulling them into line when needed. It's about getting to know them early, being fair and looking for opportunities to express joy and humour. We are teaching kids and adolescents, not enemies to be vanquished.

A bit of well-meaning advice that I received when I started teaching was to not smile until Easter, or the end of Term 1. Supposedly this would instil a touch of fear into the hearts and minds of my students. I lasted a day! I just couldn't do it. What a miserable experience to put myself and my students through. I didn't go through four years of university to become a grumpy old bloke at the age of 22. It is my belief that people become teachers because they genuinely like children and want to make a difference to their lives. When a person decides to pursue a qualification as a teacher, they don't say to themselves that they want to teach the Australian Curriculum to Year 5 boys and girls. Admittedly, many secondary teachers do have a deep love of their subject area. However, they would become disillusioned very quickly if teaching a specialist subject was their only reason for entering the profession. Their job is to instil within their students a deep love of that subject. To do this they must bring the subject to life in the hearts and minds of the students. If a kid doesn't 'get' something, it means the teacher needs to find another way to reach them. The student holds a lock, and you are the key. If the child is being an outright little pest, they are partially to blame for not 'getting' it. But that's another matter entirely!

Content knowledge is critical across all year levels and subject areas. The adage that a good teacher can teach anything is simply not true. Sure, you might be able to go outside your preferred grades or subject areas, but that stretch only extends so far. Try getting a secondary teacher to take a lower primary class, or an English teacher to take maths for a year. A teacher who knows their subject area is very valuable indeed, but their ability to impart this content is enhanced by the establishment of a relationship with their students. A student who does not like or respect you will at best not learn from you and at worst cause you grief. It doesn't matter if you have two doctorates in your subject area; this has no currency with a 13-year-old. The relationship comes first.

How do you build relationships and rapport?

Kids need to know that they come first and the subject you're teaching comes second. Be kind, thoughtful and gentle in your communication. There's enough aggression in the world, so don't add to it in your classroom. Kids might take a while to respond, but they will gradually come around. Even the more hardened kids will warm to you. And stick at it: don't be dissuaded by a terrible lesson and think you have to go all hard-arse military style on your class! There may be other things you can adjust before John Rambo is unleashed. There will be a time for raising your voice to significant octaves, but this should be your final card trick. If you use it too early and too regularly, the class will become desensitised to the volume and realise that you have no strategies left. You'll become miserable and lose your most important teaching tool: your voice.

Begin smiling on day one. A simple smile signals to another human being that you are happy to see them and be in their company. Some kids don't see too many smiles. If yours is their first for the day, that's a great start. Remember that you chose this profession. There were plenty of other options in the tertiary handbooks that you picked up at career expos. If you want to be miserable every day, go and become a lawyer!

Get to know your students. How? Before you even step into the classroom, seek out the class list and talk to a few other teachers about the kids. Have a look into their socioeconomic backgrounds. Find out what sports or hobbies they are into. Try not to get too caught up in a colleague's negativity about a student or a class. Their experience is not yours. If you go into a class with preconceived notions, your students will quickly see that you haven't given them a chance and will confirm what you have been told.

Be your own person and find your own style. What works for another teacher probably won't work for you. You can't keep a mask on lesson after lesson, day after day. I fell into this trap early in my career. Be stronger than that. Craft a teaching persona that fits your personality. Schools are bizarre places sometimes. No one will sit you down and tell you all of this. It's usually a case of here's your class list, your classroom map, your timetable, your school calendar, your desk, your laptop if you're lucky and off you go!

Reach out to parents early and often. Most schools have a database, usually called a School Management System, that allows you to access contact details and send individual or bulk emails. I recommend sending a bulk email to all parents at the start of the year to introduce yourself and give a bit of a background on your subjects, topics and key dates. This achieves a few things. First, it starts to build a relationship between school and home. A secondary student will often have several teachers, so introducing yourself in a more personalised way is a good idea. You don't want your first communication with parents to happen mid-year. An email also signals to the parents and the child that you care, have taken the time to reach out and want success for all your students. Last of all, it covers your backside. A parent can never say that they haven't received any communication from school or from you as a teacher. Nor can they say that they haven't been given an opportunity to have a conversation with you about a concern they may have. You'll be surprised how much goodwill a nicely crafted bulk email will attract, and it's something you'll continue to draw upon as the year unfolds. Send out an email to parents at least once a term.

The next step in the communication tango is an email or a phone call to a parent whose child is being particularly disrespectful, or is at risk of underperforming or failing. Depending on school policy, you may need to get some advice from your line manager first. (This person's title could be Year Level Coordinator, Head of House, Head of Department, Deputy Principal or Head of Curriculum.) When talking to parents, keep your tone polite and factual. Make it clear that you are being proactive, care enough to let them know of your concerns and want to work together towards improvement. After this intervention, the student will either improve or continue to spiral. If further consequences need to be applied, they will not come as a surprise for parents or child. This approach will demonstrate to your line manager that you've proactively tried to find a solution. Do not talk yourself out of making that phone call if you think a parent will become aggressive or deflect blame. This may indeed happen, but not calling is the worst thing you can do.

If you are able, get involved in activities such as camps, tours, excursions and coaching or managing teams. This will build your relationships with students away from your subject area. You'll have conversations, you'll learn about them and they'll learn about you. Teaching is much more than what occurs inside the four walls of the classroom. The sooner you understand this, the more joy you will have.

Three key points from this chapter

1. Relationships come before subject content
2. Start smiling on your first day
3. Communicate regularly with parents

2

Planning and the five Ps

Whenever I have a poor lesson—and there have been plenty—it is often due to a lack of prior planning. It never ceases to amaze me how little planning some teachers do. These same teachers wonder why the students in their class are either half asleep or playing up like a second-hand car. My simple tip is to learn the five Ps: prior planning prevents poor performance.

Let's break this down a little bit. 'Prior' doesn't mean just before a lesson. Sure, there may be times when extenuating circumstances turn your presence at school into a minor miracle. I'm not talking about those days when turning up against all odds alleviates the need for admin to find a replacement teacher. On those days you might have to wing it or set some rather dull work to keep the kids busy and hopefully settled. A 10-minute planning job will be as good as it gets. If you have a good relationship with your students, they will work with you to get through the day. In other words, you will trade on the relationship and rapport that you've already established.

But this should be the exception to the rule. A lack of prior planning lets down your students, your colleagues and your profession. If you want to be treated as a professional and get paid accordingly, then act like it.

Prior planning is more than just an investment of time. It means thinking deeply about the students in your class, the content to be delivered and the resources, tools, strategies and experiences that you will use.

Prior planning will vary across the stages of your career. A rookie needs to plan more thoroughly than a 30-year veteran does. Early-career teachers still lack classroom experience and a deep understanding of content, assessment and classroom management. My preparation for units, topics and individual lessons is still extensive at times. It becomes more or less detailed based on my experience with the topic and content.

Planning not only helps you deliver a killer lesson, but also has a domino effect that is impossible to measure. This effect travels across the school year and sometimes beyond. Students, parents and colleagues alike will have confidence in you as a teacher. They will know what is happening now and what is coming up. It's a beautiful thing! Who would have thought that someone could get all misty-eyed about planning? Spend enough time in a school and your reputation for planning will precede you and make things easier. The flip side is that a lack of planning will also become common knowledge, and everyone will respond accordingly.

Planning gives you a road map for lessons and units of work. It gives you assurance and certainty, brings balance to a lesson, and instils confidence and clarity in your students (even if they don't call it that). It reduces your stress and ultimately brings success to your students. A teacher who doesn't plan is quite simply arrogant and irresponsible—certainly not someone I'd want on my staff.

Short-term planning

Also known as micro planning, to be used for individual lessons. A PE lesson might involve learning how to dribble a basketball. A history lesson might explore the origins of World War I. A geography lesson might identify different types of tectonic plates. Your planning should include very targeted details, sometimes even rough timings as to when to start and finish a topic or activity. It could also include names of students and what they might need from you, especially if you're providing some extension or consolidation work for them. My short-term planning in

February has very little reference or connection to what I might be doing in October. I will know what I am doing in October, and some skills taught at the start of the year might be used later in the year, but that is all part of my long-term plan.

Medium-term planning

Use this for a week's worth of lessons, a unit of work, a term or a semester. A week may cover 2 to 5 lessons. A unit may be as short as 4 weeks or as long as 20 weeks. A term is 8 to 11 weeks, and a semester is 2 terms or 16 to 22 weeks in Australia. Preparation will involve both micro and macro planning. A unit of work is generally a defined piece of content or a topic with a culminating piece of assessment. For example, a unit of work for Year 7 Basketball will include game fundamentals such as dribbling, passing, shooting, rules and positions. It will include some time to put these elements together, perhaps among two or three teammates. It will also include some offensive and defensive strategies, and finally game time. It might also be paired with a theory unit on basic exercise physiology and energy systems or anatomy. This will usually go for at least a term and will culminate in some type of assessment.

Long-term planning

Also known as macro planning, this covers an entire school year. You'll need to map out the entire year of work for a specific class or year level, often per subject area. For Year 10 Business I would expect to plan for each topic, specifying the length of time and the assessment required. Mapping out assessment dates would allow me to give myself time to cover the content, mark the assessment and complete the reports. I would also look at what had been done prior to Year 10, and what students would need to know if they chose Business in Year 11 and 12. A year level and a subject are not isolated islands: they sit within a continuum of year levels and a collection of subjects. A good Head of Department or Head of Teaching and Learning will pull all of this together, make the connections clear and sequential, and establish a map covering the whole school, the subject area or the curriculum.

Practical planning tips

Short-term

There are dozens of templates available online to help you structure a lesson. Simply choose one that resonates with you. I'd want to see the following:

- **Basics at the top:** year level, subject or topic, date
- **Focus:** what is the purpose of this lesson?
- **Objectives:** what do you want to achieve by the end of this lesson?
- **Materials:** what resources do you require for this lesson? Laptops, worksheets, a data projector, tennis racquets, frogs for dissections?
- **Format, structure and steps:** the lesson must have an opening, a body and a conclusion

These are the guts of your lesson, so let's spend a bit of time here. A typical lesson will go for 50 minutes, so your introduction and conclusion will each be approximately five minutes. Your introduction really needs to grab attention. Think about how you'll do this: a visual, a story, a link to a previous lesson? You'll need high energy and clear wording. Your conclusion needs to wrap it all up. Check their understanding, plan for the next lesson or look to the upcoming assessment piece.

The body of your lesson needs some fleshing out. What content will you be covering and what activities, tasks or methods will you use to deliver this content? Teaching approaches that I particularly like include the Gradual Release of Responsibility model; the I Do, We Do, You Do approach; and the Guided Practice, Independent Practice model (Fisher & Frey, 2021). These allow for teacher-led instruction, supervised student practice and student-led independent work. If you can get through all of this in one lesson every time, you have a gift! Now, let's get back to short-term planning.

- **Differentiations or adjustments:** you might need to include notes around support or extension work and activities for an individual or a group of students. (See Chapter 13 for more information.)

- **Reflection or evaluation:** I recommend writing a note-to-self on what worked and what didn't. You could reflect on a student or a learning tool. You might also make connections to upcoming assessment pieces or projects.
- **Homework:** you may include planning for this separately or in your conclusion.

Here are two samples of basic and detailed short-term planning that I created myself. Names are all fictional.

Simple lesson plan for Year 2: Thinking About Time

This could be used for a lesson teaching Year 2 kids how to tell the time. The key headings within each box are quite standard and work well for me. Anyone who picks up this plan can clearly see what they are expected to do and how they will get it done. You'll notice that there is nothing about a seating plan or behaviour management strategies, which you might need to add. Adjust according to your class and the students themselves. Take into account the ages of the kids, the layout of the classroom and the work you may have already put in.

Who, what, where and when	Lesson focus
Class: Year 2 Topic: Thinking About Time Location: Room A101 Date: Fri 23 Feb Length: 50 minutes	How do patterns in numbers help us tell time?

Objectives	Materials and resources
I would like my students to be able to tell the time to the hour by the end of this lesson.	Demo clock for teacher Student cardboard clocks in pairs Printable clocks per student Story problem cards Whiteboard Coloured pencils

	Lesson format	
Intro: 5 minutes	Get their attention and tell them what we are about to learn	
	Who has seen one of these before? (Hold up a clock.)	
	How many numbers can you see? Let's count them together.	
	Did you know that there are 24 hours in the day? 12 hours in the morning and 12 hours in the afternoon? Today we are going to learn how to tell the time.	
	(Note: this lesson will not focus on am & pm.)	
Body: Part A	Give each child their own printed clock. They can draw on this.	
	Discuss with them: little hand tells the hour, big hand tells the minute.	
	Key terms: second, minute, hour.	
	Key points: 60 seconds per minute & 60 minutes per hour.	
	Count it out with them as a whole class.	
Body: Part B	Teacher demo on whiteboard: 3 o'clock, 6 o'clock, 9 o'clock, 12 o'clock. (Have four clocks ready to go.)	
	Reinforce the position of the little hand and the big hand.	
	Guided practice: with teacher help, students use their printed sheets to write 1 o'clock through to 12 o'clock. Write the times in different colours where possible.	
	In pairs: students use their cardboard clocks to physically move clock hands. Teacher calls out times such as 4 o'clock, 11 o'clock and so forth.	
Body: Part C	Dependent on time and progress in Parts A and B.	
	Teacher demo first: read out a scenario for the class to solve together. Do this a few times.	
	Give students a scenario to solve themselves.	
	(Sample scenario: Helen has a ballet lesson in one hour. It is 4 o'clock right now. When does her ballet lesson start?)	
Conclusion: 5 minutes	Get their attention back again and reinforce.	
	All eyes on teacher: reinforce as a whole class.	
	How many hours in a day? How many minutes per hour? How many seconds per minute?	
	When does school start (9 o'clock)? Show me.	
	When does school finish (3 o'clock)? Show me.	

Differentiation		
Consolidation	**Core**	**Complexity**
Focus on big hand and little hand. Big hand is the minute hand, little hand is the hour hand. Provide simple scenarios. Focus on 3, 6, 9 and 12 o'clock on printable sheets.	As per lesson plan. 1 o'clock through to 12 o'clock. Tell time to the hour. Use printable sheets. Basic terms. Provide a range of scenarios.	Provide more complex scenarios to solve. Or give them a scenario with a half-hour inclusion.

Homework	**Reflection**
In your homework books there are eight circles. Draw the following: Show me 2, 4, 6, 8 o'clock. Show me 6.30, 7.30, 10.30, 11.30.	

Detailed lesson plan for Year 8: Health, Nutrition and Food Groups

Here I have kept the fundamentals of a lesson plan in place but added significantly more detail, particularly to the body of the lesson. I've added a seating plan and some fake names to show how you may need to cater for individual kids. You will notice that I've included a variety of activities. This will generate interest, encourage the kids to contribute and allow for a mix of learning styles. I'm not cramming too much into this lesson. It's Year 8 and I have 50 minutes. This is a large class with mixed abilities, so by the time I get the kids seated and settled I'll have 45 minutes. If I don't get through all this content then I'll carry it over to the next lesson. The student names aren't real, but this is a lesson that I have taught dozens of times.

Who, what, where and when	Lesson focus
Class: Year 8A Topic: Health, Nutrition and Food Groups Location: D101 Date: Tue 23 October Length: 50 minutes	The five food groups and key nutrients. This lesson won't focus on the recommended amount of each food group that should be consumed per day. That will be next lesson. It will also introduce the nutrients, but it won't explore the purpose of each nutrient.

Objectives	Materials and resources
By the end of this lesson, I would like my students to know the five food groups, some sample foods from each and the nutrients derived from these.	Task sheets Data projector Student laptops

Lesson format	
Intro: 5 minutes	Get their attention and tell them what we are about to learn. Start with a visual of a bodybuilder on the data projector. This is an extreme example that will get their attention. The discussion will be on the key food groups and nutrients needed to build muscle. The next photo will be of a long-distance runner. The final photo will be of a rugby league player. Again, lead the same discussion around the respective food groups and nutrients needed to fuel performance. Our focus today is on two things: food groups and key nutrients from these foods. Remember the 5 & 6 rule: five food groups and six nutrients.
Body Part A: 5 minutes	Brainstorming activity: what are the food groups? Write them on the board. Expect all sorts of things to be thrown up. Once complete, circle the five food groups in different colours.<ul><li>Vegetables</li><li>Fruit</li><li>Grains</li><li>Meat, fish and poultry</li><li>Dairy</li></ul>

Body Part B: 10 minutes	Explore examples for each of these five food groups: - Vegetables: beans, carrots, pumpkin, potato, celery, onion, broccoli - Fruit: apple, orange, banana, grape, pineapple - Grains: bread, oats, rice, quinoa, cereal - Meat, fish and poultry: beef, chicken, fish, duck, turkey, lamb - Dairy: milk, yoghurt, cheese Each student can have a printed sheet of a plate that is split into five segments. Write each food group, then add examples to each. Teacher models this on the whiteboard or in a PowerPoint produced earlier. *8 minutes* Watch a video about the food groups. I recommend 'Exploring the Five Food Groups' on the *Healthy Eating* YouTube channel. While the video is playing, students can complete the accompanying task sheet and answer the questions. *5 minutes* Once the video has finished, go over the task sheet answers with the students.
Body Part C: 10 minutes	A quick brainstorm around the nutrients obtained from foods. Write it on the board. Six in total: - Protein - Carbohydrates - Fats - Vitamins - Minerals - Water Now give a few examples of types of food that provide each of these nutrients. Some Q&A with the kids. - Protein: meat, tofu, fish - Carbohydrates: rice, millet, oats - Fats: oils, fried foods, salami, yoghurt - Vitamins: A, D, K - Minerals: calcium, sodium, potassium - Water: from the tap, some fruits Teacher writes examples on board. Students write them on printed sheet.

Body Part C (cont.)	**If time allows** Student exploration using own laptops. Using as an example the foods listed above, answer what provides the following: • Vitamins A, D and K • Calcium, sodium, potassium Sample answer: calcium is found in yoghurt, vitamin A in leafy green vegetables. Have task sheet ready to distribute.
Conclusion: 5 minutes	Get their attention back and reinforce Recap the 5 & 6 rule Quiz students about some foods and the nutrients these contain Next lesson will focus on the role that each nutrient plays in the body (such as protein building muscle) and recommended daily intakes

Differentiation		
Consolidation	**Core**	**Complexity**
Focus on the 5 & 6 rule. Use simple graphic organiser to write these out and provide one example for each. Yunus and James will need additional support.	As per lesson plan. Complete the task sheets as per instructions.	Students can explore additional vitamins and minerals and the purpose of these. For example: Vitamin B12 comes from sardines and helps produce red blood cells. Check on Emma and her progress.

Homework	Reflection
Share another video on the food groups, to be summarised in 50 words. I recommend 'Food Group Superheroes: Make-A-Plate THIS or THAT (Balanced Diet Activity)' from the *NETFLEX Kids: Studio* YouTube channel.	

Seating plan: Year 8A

Medium-term

When preparing a unit of work, I simply start with a piece of paper and a pencil. I map the unit out in a grid-like format with lessons per week and the number of weeks. I add my assessment tasks into the date or week that they are due. I'll then work backwards from those dates. I start to slot in the topics per lesson on this grid. I add bits, remove bits, make sure I cover the necessary content and have prepped the kids for assessment, and provide some time for feedback at the end. Once I'm happy with that scrappy outline I will type it up and start to flesh it out. It's creative, organic and balanced. Within this plan you can add things like guest speakers, incursions and excursions.

Simple unit plan for Year 10: Business Model Canvas

This is a real class and subject that I taught only recently. The sample is a unit of work that covers a 10-week school term. There are 2 lessons per week, so bar any public holidays or school events I should have 20 lessons in total. Once I know the topic, my thinking always turns to the assessment. Once I have that conceptualised in my mind, I'll think about what the class needs to know in order to successfully complete the subject.

In this instance the students had to produce a business model canvas, a one-page strategy that mapped out their entire business model.

Year 10 Business, Term 2: Business Model Canvas		
2 lessons per week: Monday and Thursday		
Week	Lesson 1	Lesson 2
1	*Overview of unit* Types of business models The purpose of a business model	*Business model canvas (BMC)* Explore its key features, benefits and layout with examples of a product, a consumable and a service. For example, a sport shoe, a doughnut, a massage etc.
2	*Value propositions* What they are, how to establish them, why they're important, examples. Base the activity on three examples provided. The product could be a doughnut infused with flavour of your choice.	*Key activities and key partners* How to establish and maintain them. For example, doughnut sales: various sizes, toppings, infusions; local bakery supplier and ingredient wholesaler.
3	*Customer relationships and customer segments* What they are, how to establish them, why they're important, examples. For example, a breakfast customer segment vs a dessert customer segment.	*Channels and key resources* What they are, how to establish them, why they're important, examples. For example: online orders, walk-up orders, businesses, local deliveries.
4	*Revenue streams* What they are, how to establish them, why they're important, examples. Online, in-store, deliveries, personal, corporate, parties, businesses, events etc.	*Cost structures* What they are, how to establish them, why they're important, examples. One to a dozen; dependent upon infusions etc.

Week	Lesson 1	Lesson 2
5	*Design your own BMC* Role-modelling by teacher: use a scenario of a new soft drink, shoes or a service like personal training or dog walking.	Students create their own BMC with teacher help
6	Students work on their BMC towards their assessment	Students work on their BMC towards their assessment
7	Students work on their BMC towards their assessment	Assignment draft due
8	Provide feedback to students	Work on feedback in class
9	Work on feedback in class	Assignment due: final copy
10	Return marks and formal feedback	Prep for next unit of work

Long-term

The Australian Year 9 HASS curriculum asks us to cover four subject areas: History, Geography, Civics and Business. Typically there will be 4 lessons per week if each lesson is roughly 50 minutes long. For the History component we are asked to explore world history topics from 1750 to 1918. There are three topics to be covered: 'The Industrial Revolution (1750-1914)', 'Australia and Asia' and 'World War I'. For Geography we are asked to study two units of work: 'Biomes and Food Security' and 'Geographies of Interconnectedness' (whatever that means!). For Civics we have 'Government and Democracy', 'Laws and Citizens' and 'Citizenship, Diversity and Identity'. For Business there needs to be at least one unit that explains the concept of economy, Asian and Australian economies, and the global economy.

That's a lot to cover in one year, so you've got to map it all out. We have nine topics to cover across four subject areas known collectively as HASS. We have four lessons or the equivalent per week. We have 9 or 10 weeks per term to fit it into. Each topic needs to be developed into a unit of work also known as medium-term planning. One approach could be to cover the History units in Term 1 before hitting Geography in Term 2, Civics in Term 3 and Business in Term 4.

Simple long-term or annual plan for Year 9: HASS (History and Social Sciences)

In this example you'll see less detail but you will see signposts. These signposts are the topic and the assessment, noting in particular where the assessment falls in relation to reporting periods. Long-term planning allows you to see the topics being covered, the variety of assessment methods used and the key dates. It is also useful when all grades for a subject are collated, providing a nice overview across year levels to ensure that core content is being covered.

For the assessment, you should use a variety of methods. For History I'd suggest a mixture of exam and assignment with some source analysis. For Geography you could do a project accompanied by a verbal presentation. I'd try to combine both units into one assessment piece. For Civics a multi-model presentation might be worthwhile. You could combine the three units and just do one piece of assessment. For Business, a group task or project to finish the year would work well. Term 4 is a 9-week term. Assessment would generally need to be done by Week 7 to allow for end-of-year reports, award ceremonies and the start of Year 10 work.

A more thorough syllabus or program of work is provided in the Australian Curriculum. This example is basic, but that's the whole point. It's something you should refer to regularly. Place it at the front of your folder of work to keep you on track. This is one of the first things that I want to see as a principal when I ask a teacher to show me their planning. It shows me that you've thought about the timing of your units of work and worked out the assessment.

Term	Unit or topic	Assessment method	Notes
1 (10 weeks)	*History* Industrial Revolution (Weeks 1–4) Asian & Australian society 1750–1918 (Weeks 5–7) WWI & Australia's involvement (Weeks 8–10)	Exam: multiple choice & short answer (Week 7) Assignment (Week 10)	May combine the exams so that there are 2 pieces of assessment for the term
2 (10 weeks)	*Geography* Biomes (Weeks 1–4) Geographies of Interconnectedness (Weeks 5 – 9)	Project with verbal component (Week 9)	Sem 1 reports due in Week 10
3 (10 weeks)	*Civics* Government & Democracy Laws & Citizens Citizenship, Diversity & Identity (combined unit over 9 weeks)	Multi-model project (Week 9)	Year 9 camp in Week 5
4 (9 weeks)	*Business* Economy, Australian economy, global economy (Weeks 1-7)	Assignment: create your own business (Week 7)	Sem 2 reports due in Week 8

I start with a wide planning lens and narrow it down. First I build my yearly long-term plan, then I create medium-term unit plans as I approach them on the calendar, then I do short-term planning the week or day before a lesson. You don't have to get all your unit plans done at the start of the year, especially if you are rolling out a new curriculum or have picked up a new year level. Stay ahead of the kids, but don't push yourself to be nine months ahead!

Three key points from this chapter

1. If you want to have some success at the teaching game, get comfortable with planning
2. If you fail to plan, you plan to fail
3. Start long, then medium, then short—planning, that is!

3
Theories, models and frameworks: making sense of the education jungle

When I was going through university, I kept hearing about key people who had influenced educational thinking. Sometimes it was just a single surname like Vygotsky or Piaget, and we students were supposed to somehow know this person's impressive contribution to teaching and learning. Sometimes I wasn't even sure if it was a real name or some Latin derivative meant to impress us undergraduates. Sometimes the name took on its own aura and morphed into a framework, model or theory: Bloom's Taxonomy of Learning Domains, Kolb's Four Stages of Experiential Learning, Bandura's Social Learning Theory. By the way, when does a framework become a model or theory? One of life's great mysteries. Names like Dewey, Gagné, de Bono, Pavlov, Skinner, Bruner… there are dozens of them, all morphed together in the great maelstrom of educational theories and theorists.

But no one—and I emphasise, no one!—ever explained who all these people were, what they had contributed or how schools used the theory or model or whatever it was that they invented. My suspicion is that our lecturers didn't know. Perhaps it was all too unwieldy and there was ambiguity or disagreement around what school of thought these theorists belonged to. Perhaps they simply hadn't spent enough time in a classroom to know about the raw realities of teaching students. Trust me, Vygotsky is the last thing on my mind when I am planning or teaching. Yes, names like Pavlov (and his dog) were sprinkled throughout our lectures, but no one ever pulled everything together to provide an overview or potted history.

So we are left with teachers across the country (and quite possibly the world) who have absolutely no idea about the educational thinkers of their own profession, how these people impacted teaching or if anything they are known for actually makes a difference in the classroom. Most teachers have heard of Benjamin Bloom and many have heard of Bill Rogers, but few of us would realise that both men built on the work of others before them: Robert M. Gagné in the case of Bloom, and Ivan Pavlov in the case of Rogers. And how many would know that Socrates was the teacher of Plato, and both fall into the category of humanism which later inspired the work of Carl Rogers and the formation of the student-centred learning approach?

Knowing all of this won't have any effect on your planning for next week. However, these people are pioneers in the profession to which we have chosen to dedicate our lives. Furthermore, theories play a big role in how we teach and in our understanding of how students learn. For better or worse, these theories have shaped how school buildings are designed, how assessment is created and how content is delivered. Bloom's Taxonomy is the basis upon which most assessment criteria is structured: from basic knowledge through to the analysis and application of this knowledge, and finally to the evaluation of a product, process or feature. We've all heard of lower-order and higher-order thinking—that too is derived from Bloom's Taxonomy. John Dewey is the original architect of self-directed learning. Abraham Maslow coined the phrase 'hierarchy of needs', a concept now well entrenched in school wellbeing programs.

I have summarised these theorists, theories, models, frameworks and taxonomies into a framework of my own. I call it an ecosystem, because our understanding of how we teach and how we learn is constantly evolving.

There are undoubtedly some significant people whom I have left out—this is not by design or due to any philosophical vendetta on my behalf! I've decided that categories like this are a bit like debating the best athlete or sporting team in history: it's impossible to judge. I have placed theories and theorists into categories where I think they best fit.

Four major learning theories

Constructivism

This theory says that learners construct knowledge rather than passively taking in information. As people experience the world and reflect upon those experiences, they build their own understanding and incorporate new information into their pre-existing knowledge.

Cognitivism

This theory focuses on how information is received, organised, stored and retrieved by the mind. The brain is used as an information processer like a computer. Cognitivism looks beyond observable behaviour, viewing learning as an internal mental process.

Behaviourism

This theory holds that all behaviours are learned through interaction with the environment and that innate, genetic or inherited factors have very little influence on behaviour. In terms of nature vs nurture, this is all nurture.

Humanism

This theory is based on our reasoning ability and common humanity. It takes the approach that values are established through human nature and experiences. Humanistic learning is student-centred, so students are encouraged to take control over their education. They make choices on everything from daily activities to future goals.

From learning theories to frameworks

All models, frameworks, steps, phases, stages, theories, scaffolds and environments can be traced back to one of the big four educational approaches previously listed.

Theorists align themselves with these respective categories according to how they believe people learn. Models produced by theorists dictate how we should teach, which then leads to thinking frameworks, learning frameworks and methods of instruction.

To capture this, I have established four levels starting with the major categories and narrowing towards specific teaching tools:

- **Level 1.** Learning theory categories and the prominent theorists attached to each category
- **Level 2.** Learning models created by these theorists
- **Level 3.** Learning environments derived from a specific model or theory
- **Level 4.** Learning frameworks established from or inspired by a specific model or theory

Think of Levels 1 and 2 as the theoretical positions on how we learn, and of Levels 3 and 4 as the practical applications of these theories with the tools or strategies created to enact them.

You will now be able to speak very broadly on teaching and learning theories with some intelligence and authority. Just imagine being at your next staff meeting and John from Humanities tells everyone that Bloom was a behaviourist. *Well actually, John, he was most commonly thought of as a cognitivist. This is really quite easy to see due to the way he believed information is accessed, understood and applied by the human brain. I mean a taxonomy is a dead giveaway, surely...*

Now wouldn't that be a hoot!

Our learning ecosystem

Level 1. Learning theory categories: how we believe learning is achieved			
Constructivism	Cognitivism	Behaviourism	Humanism
Prominent theorists attached to each learning theory category			
Jean Piaget Albert Bandura John Dewey Lev Vygotsky David Kolb	Françoys Gagne Jerome Bruner Howard Gardner John Flavell Benjamin Bloom	Ivan Pavlov B.F. Skinner Dugan Laird Rudolf Dreikurs Lee Canter Bill Rogers	Carl Rogers Socrates Erik Erikson Abraham Maslow Maria Montessori Rudolf Steiner
Level 2. Learning models: how we operationalise and apply these theories			
Vygotsky: scaffolding; zone of proximal development Piaget: schema; stages of cognitive development Kolb: 4 stages of experiential learning Dewey: experiential learning; social learning; inquiry-based learning, self-directed learning Bandura: social learning theory	Bloom: domains of learning; Bloom's Taxonomy Gardner: multiple intelligences Gagne: 5 conditions of learning; 9 levels of learning; model of giftedness and talent Bruner: spiral curriculum; 3 modes of representation Flavell: metacognition	Pavlov: classical conditioning Skinner: operant conditioning; positive reinforcement Laird: sensory theory Canter: assertive discipline Bill Rogers: behaviour management guru Dreikurs: classroom management theory	Erikson: 8 stages of psychological development Carl Rogers: student-centred learning Maslow: hierarchy of needs Socrates: father of philosophy and teacher of Plato Montessori and Steiner: whole-person learning

Theories, models and frameworks: making sense of the education jungle

Level 3. Learning environments: how we set up our environments and relationships for learning

Maslow: hierarchy of needs

Erikson: 8 stages of psychological development

Dewey: inquiry-based learning & self-directed learning

Canter, Bill Rogers and Dreikurs: classroom environment and management

Bloom: domains of learning

Seligman: PERMA and positive education

Level 4. Learning frameworks: the scaffolds we create to structure learning across organisations and classrooms

4a. Teaching frameworks	4b. Thinking frameworks	4c. Methods of instruction
The Art and Science of Teaching (Marzano) *Dimensions of Learning* (Marzano & Pickering) Technological Pedagogical Content Knowledge (Mishra & Koehler) *Teachers and Productive Pedagogies* (Lingard et al.) SAMR Model (Puentedura)	Habits of Mind (Costa and Kallick) Bloom's Taxonomy (Bloom) SOLO Taxonomy (Biggs & Collis) Six Thinking Hats (de Bono) Multiple Intelligences (Gardner) Cultures of Thinking and Visible Thinking (Harvard Project Zero)	Direct instruction: otherwise known as explicit teaching or I Do, We Do, You Do Indirect instruction: includes project-based learning Experiential learning: student-centred Individual study: self-directed learning; individualised learning plans Interactive instruction: includes inquiry-based learning; links to thinking and problem-solving frameworks Flipped learning methodologies

Three key points from this chapter

1. The four main categories of learning theories are constructivism, cognitivism, behaviourism and humanism
2. Every theorist aligns with one of these categories
3. Every major framework, model and method of instruction can be traced back to these categories and theorists

4
Methods of instruction: what to use and when to use it

It is interesting to hear teachers talk about the universal superiority of their preferred method of instruction. I find this frankly bewildering. A method of instruction is like a tool that you pick off a shelf to use for a particular purpose. No one tool is better than another. You wouldn't always choose a hammer over a screwdriver, would you? If you need to tighten a screw then a hammer is not your friend. Teachers need to choose methods that suit students, classes, content and tasks. A teacher who refuses to adjust an obviously unsuitable method ought to be sacked. These teachers are at best arrogant and dangerous, at worst incompetent and dangerous!

One purpose of the educational machine is to instil in young people some skills and attributes needed for them to function in work and in life. Fostering these skills and attributes in the early years will facilitate success in Years 11 and 12. When seeking to apply methods of instruction that best suit the child and the class, we should have one eye on what these children will need for their respective futures.

Six methods of instruction

Teaching methods can be divided into six categories. Warning: teachers can get confused, bewildered and sometimes argumentative about these categories, which people in their wisdom have given different names over the years.

1. Direct instruction, also called explicit teaching
2. Indirect instruction, also called inquiry-based or exploratory learning
3. Experiential learning, also called active or project-based learning
4. Interactive instruction, also called collaborative learning
5. Individual study, also called self-directed learning
6. Flipped learning (believe it or not, that's its only name)

At the end of the day, it doesn't really matter what you call them. If you prefer direct instruction but a colleague prefers explicit teaching, who really cares. All that matters is that you know what they are and which tools they typically require.

For each method or category there are instructional tools or strategies. A teacher's choice of tool may depend on their level of comfort, the dynamics of the classroom and where they are in a term or a unit of work. A typical tool used for the method of instruction commonly called project-based learning is an excursion. A lecture might be used for direct instruction, and a case study for indirect instruction.

Methods of instruction: tools and purposes for teaching and learning

The tables in the following pages identify three tools for each method, with commentary around usage. I have provided 18 tools as examples, but in reality there are dozens more.

Direct instruction or explicit teaching

Instructional tool	Purpose (why & when)	Planning consideration (pre-lesson)	Delivery consideration (in-lesson)
Definition: Prepared and led by the teacher. Involves an explicit, carefully sequenced and scripted model of instruction.			
I Do, We Do, You Do	Part of a clear continuum of teaching and great when teaching a specific skill or piece of content.	If applied in a single lesson, think about the time given for each of the 3 sections. A great method for teaching a specific formula or a discreet technique.	Don't get absorbed in the 'I Do' section, must give kids time to practice.
Lecture, seminar, discussion	To deliver content when didactic methodology is best. Large groups, time-poor, lots of content.	Unless you are a dynamic speaker or have content that makes the audience hang on every word, think about techniques beyond 'chalk and talk'.	Mix up your delivery style to avoid boredom. Add some media or slides to augment dialogue, explore opportunities for audience interaction.
Practice and revision or recitation	Perfect when a formula, event or technique needs to be firmly embedded in the mind of the learner.	Give kids the 'why'. Why does this need to be remembered, how will it be of benefit, how can it be applied to different scenarios?	At the end of the lesson, think about how you will check what has been remembered. How well was it embedded?

Indirect instruction, inquiry-based learning or exploratory learning

Instructional tool	Purpose (why & when)	Planning consideration (pre-lesson)	Delivery consideration (in-lesson)
Definition: Student-centred. An emphasis on critical and higher-order thinking. The teacher takes on the role of facilitator.			
Problem-solving	Need to apply what has been learned to a different problem or scenario. The class demo is the easy part, but can it be applied to a different issue? Build this into the lesson.	Have some problems ready to go. Have different problems of varying complexity so that all learners are challenged.	Frame it up for the class and role model it. Do an 'I Do, We Do, You Do' first and then let them loose.
Case studies	Applies what has been taught to a new context. A case study is authentic and real-world with tangible benefit.	As above. Have some case studies ready to go, the more authentic the better.	Explain the case, give some background. Then do similar to above.
Reflective discussion or group discussion	Explore different perspectives on a topic so that listening is emphasised, humility and consideration are encouraged.	Think about grouping size and composition.	Give some boundaries to the discussion, some protocols. Have ready-made questions, put time limits and outcomes in place.

Experiential instruction, active learning or project-based learning

Instructional tool	Purpose (why & when)	Planning consideration (pre-lesson)	Delivery consideration (in-lesson)
Definition: The process of learning through experience is active, as opposed to didactic learning.			
Adventure-based learning or team-building activities	Hands-on. Learn through trial and error, challenge and adversity.	Significant planning involved. Must really think about the purpose of the exercise, group dynamics and safety.	Be a facilitator. Groups may find different ways to achieve the same outcome. Resist the urge to get too involved.
Excursions	Learn through observation and direct experience rather than via text or other media.	Significant, as above, although might be facilitated through a provider (e.g. zoo guide, instructor)	As the excursion or field trip unfolds, are you getting out of it what you need? Is it meeting the learning goals? Are the kids safe?
Drama, Art, Theatre, Hospitality, PE, Technology, Science	Inherently practical subjects in nature. Learn through doing.	Significant, as above. Each subject will have its own risks and each class will have its own dynamics to manage.	Be comfortable in chaos but have a plan. Give kids the structure and expectations in advance then be consistent in the application of these.

Interactive instruction or collaborative learning

Instructional tool	Purpose (why & when)	Planning consideration (pre-lesson)	Delivery consideration (in-lesson)
Definition: Relies heavily on discussion and sharing among participants. Students learn from their peers just as much as from their teacher.			
Debates	Collaboration and communication. Gives structure but encourages problem-solving, developing an argument, defending a point, teamwork under pressure.	What is the topic? Who are the team members? What are their roles? Does everyone know the debate protocols?	Prepare a list of simple rules for the debate and distribute beforehand. Include a reminder that students participating in the debate and audience should not disrupt speakers.
Jigsaw	Allows specialisation and then teaching that skill or knowledge to others.	Significant. Must plan the specific parts or jigsaw pieces, then consider how these will be brought together.	An excellent method that builds individual accountability and achievement of team goals, so think carefully about group mix and dynamics.
Think, Pair, Share	Encourages every student to participate in learning rather than being passive.	Can be changed to Think, Pair, Square if students are nervous about sharing in front of a whole class. They can just share to another group of 3 or 4.	Allows the teacher to change a traditional whole-class discussion into a more manageable and personalised activity.

Individual study or self-directed learning

Instructional tool	Purpose (why & when)	Planning consideration (pre-lesson)	Delivery consideration (in-lesson)
Definition: An activity undertaken by a learner with little or no supervision.			
Individualised learning plans	Used when each individual student needs a specific plan to support their unique needs.	Data to inform planning. Feedback to inform planning. Input from specialists or parents.	Provide time for reflection, reinforcement and exploration of interests.
Distance learning	Geographical challenges. Physical challenges. Social/emotional challenges.	Technology: is it sufficient to support the learning goals and intentions?	Methods of communication must be varied: videoconferencing, email, Canvas/Moodle. Should have both visual and verbal comms.
Self-directed learning	The individual can decide what to focus on.	Must establish the skills and tools to do SDL effectively. It takes time and should be sequentially developed.	Checking in: how and when? Don't just leave them to their own devices.

Flipped learning methodologies

Instructional tool	Purpose (why & when)	Planning consideration (pre-lesson)	Delivery consideration (in-lesson)
Definition: Replaces teacher instruction with video or pre-lesson tasks. Students then apply what they learned in class with teacher working as a coach or guide, or responding to questions. The key here is that the content is absorbed before the lesson, and the lesson is an opportunity for clarification and Q&A.			
A video or text, to be done pre-lesson. Add an ability to review and reflect on content with a tool such as Padlet.	Allows students to work at their own pace.	Internet access, a suitable study environment at home. The ability to get the work done prior to the lesson.	Students must have done the pre-work.
A video followed by a formative quiz or assessment using something like Quizizz.	Allows students to determine for themselves the content they need to review.	It helps if students are motivated enough to do the work themselves prior to the lesson.	Keep the pre-work within the lesson. Build it into the unit plan and lesson plans.
A learning management system such as Google Classroom, Moodle, Blackboard or Canvas.	Provides a great deal of flexibility and potentially creates time in the lesson for deeper learning.	There's nothing more frustrating for the kids than the links or media not working. Check before directing the class to them.	It's difficult when some students have done the pre-work and some haven't. This will need to be catered for within the lesson.

From teacher-led to student-led

A useful way to visualise methods of instruction is as a continuum from top-down teaching to self-directed learning.

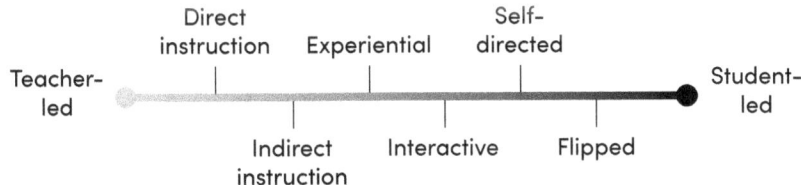

As you can see, there is a very clear transition from teacher-led methods through to student-led methods. We start off with the teacher doing most of the talking and content dissemination, telling students what to do and when to do it. Zero student choice. In the student-led or flipped model, teacher prepares for the lesson but is uninvolved or minimally involved in the lesson itself. It is up to the students to determine pace and even direction.

I always start with direct instruction when I embark on a unit of work or an individual lesson. I like to set my students up with clear expectations. Depending on class dynamics, content, complexity and assessment, I will gradually release control and move towards student-directed or flipped learning. I'll pepper my lessons with all sorts of methods and tools; some will work, some won't. The success of these methods and tools dictates how quickly we move towards the student-led end of the continuum (if we get there at all).

Early-career teachers will often err on the side of direct instruction for a greater sense of control and authority. There's nothing wrong with direct instruction, as long as it's not done all lesson every lesson. At some point, the kids need to do the work for themselves. You do everyone a disservice if you only lecture from the front of the room. Most of your students will switch off at various stages of the lesson, some within the first minute. Mix it up a little and give those kids who learn differently a chance to connect with the content. If a tool doesn't work, it's not the end of the world.

But remember: if you fail to plan, you plan to fail. The success of your experimentations and efforts will hinge on your prior planning.

> **Three key points from this chapter**
>
> 1. Fit the method to the child
> 2. Choose tools that best suit the class, the topic and your teaching goals for the lesson
> 3. Use a variety of methods falling along the continuum from teacher-led to student-led

5
Using data to inform practice

Welcome to Prep! Now sit down and complete this test. Consider this not-uncommon scenario for a moment. We have a young child, all of roughly five years old, already consumed with excitement and fear as they enter 'big school'. For the first part of Term 1 we will hammer that child with a battery of tests. What a wonderful way to switch kids off from school life. *Guess what? You have another 12 years of this ahead of you, kiddo.* Teachers are very good at collecting data. Oh, we're world champs at it.

We use assessment and national tests like NAPLAN. We do a battery of diagnostic tests every year, especially in the primary years. Some schools collect wellbeing data—not just once a year, but once a term. We do staff surveys, parent surveys, student surveys around topics like satisfaction levels, frequency of communication and frequency of feedback. We collect a plethora of data around student attendance and the socioeconomic, cultural and ethnic backgrounds of families. We collect data on how many kids participated in sport, a music program, debating or the homework club. We know how many students use the school bus, how many walk to school and how many ride a bike or get dropped off by mum.

Schools obsess over how many kids get a leaving certificate. They crunch the numbers to see how many in their graduating class achieved an ATAR or the equivalent of a tertiary entrance score. If they have done particularly well, it's broadcast on every social media platform known to man. If they haven't done so well, things go mysteriously quiet. Collecting data isn't a problem for teachers and schools. Doing something meaningful with it is another thing altogether.

There's nothing wrong with collecting data. In fact, it is useful and necessary. The reason we collect data is ostensibly to identify and do something about weaknesses, gaps, trends and patterns. We collect data so that we know where to put our energies, resources and funds. We collect data to see how a cohort, class or student is performing. We collect data over time to gauge how a class, year level, subject, program or even a whole school is tracking from year to year.

To help you get a grasp of the types of data collected, I have compiled a few summary tables. These are very general. It's impossible to be too specific: schools will use different tests at different stages, but this will give you a good understanding.

I acknowledge the contribution of ACER (Australian Council for Educational Research), as they create and publish most of these tests and provide extensive advice around their purpose and administration.

Common diagnostic tests

Test	Year levels*	Purpose
Neale Analysis of Reading Ability (NARA)	Early Years and Primary: ages 6 to 12	To measure the accuracy, comprehension and rate of reading and reading behaviour. Named after the author Marie D. Neale.
Tests of Reading Comprehension (TORCH)	Years 3 to 10	To identify comprehension levels and measure progress. Allows teachers to compare reading abilities.

Test	Year levels*	Purpose
Prose Reading Observation, Behaviour and Evaluation (PROBE)	Ages 8 to 15	To assess reading accuracy, reading behaviour and reading comprehension. It may also be used as a measure of silent reading comprehension and listening comprehension.
Progressive Achievement Tests–Reading (PAT-R)	Comprehension PAT: Prep to Year 10 Vocabulary PAT: Years 3 to 10 Spelling PAT: Years 2 to 10	There are 3 PAT-R tests, all reading-focused. All are designed to allow teachers to monitor progress in the area being tested and to inform teaching.
Progressive Achievement Tests–Maths (PAT-M)	Years 1 to 10	To monitor progress in maths and to provide teachers with diagnostic information to inform teaching.
Pattern and Structure Assessment (PASA)	Prep to Year 2	Seeks to find out how children think about mathematical ideas underlying tasks, rather than focusing on the maths that children can or cannot do (like PAT-M does).
Social-Emotional Wellbeing (SEW) Survey	Ages 3 to 18 3 different surveys: Early Years, Primary Years, Secondary Years Questions are tailored to the age of the respondents.	Should be done annually to show development or patterns over time. Identifies the social and emotional needs of student groups, then allows for the provision of targeted support.
General Ability Test (AGAT)	Ages 7 to 16	Assesses aptitude across 5 areas: abstract, kinetic, numerical, spatial and verbal. Used to determine higher-order thinking ability. Helps identify students who require extension, entry into specialist classes, scholarships or support.

Test	Year levels*	Purpose
BRIGANCE Early Childhood	Prep and Year 1	A screening test widely used by schools to determine learning difficulties or disabilities and what level of intervention may be needed. Also used to determine suitability for enrolment. Covers literacy, science and maths.
National Assessment Program—Literacy and Numeracy (NAPLAN)	Years 3, 5, 7 and 9 Once per year. There is an assessment window in the first half of the year where all schools must complete the tests.	Provides a snapshot of a student's current reading, writing, language and numeracy skills. Allows teachers and parents to see how a child is progressing against national standards over time. Also provides schools with information about how their programs are working for a cohort and what changes need to be made.

*Note: Prep or Preparatory Year is the same as Foundation Year, the year before Year 1. Early Years is generally considered Pre-Prep through to Year 2 or 3.

In addition to running diagnostic tests, schools collect a lot of generic data. This allows us to:

- Determine state and federal government funding levels
- Plan for short- and long-term staffing and facilities
- Prepare budgets
- Ensure we have sufficient resources (e.g. desks and chairs)

Opinion surveys and academic outcomes are important because they allow school leadership to determine the efficacy of programs and adjust where necessary. I can't overstress the importance of this data. Teachers may not pay too much attention, seeing it as the responsibility of leadership. But it will certainly matter when redundancies need to be made because the teacher-student ratio is unsustainable. I have redesigned a whole-school pastoral care program based on unfavourable survey data from students and parents. Data matters!

School Data

School data	Purposes
Student enrolments	• Staffing and resourcing • State and federal government funding
Student attendance	• Student wellbeing • Reporting
Class sizes	• Staffing and resourcing • Timetabling • Support requirements
• Student-to-teacher ratio • Student-to-staff ratio	• Funding • Staffing and resourcing • Subject offerings • Timetabling
School disciplinary statistics: • Detentions • Suspensions • Exclusions • Expulsions	• Behaviour-management strategies • Identifying staff needing assistance • Student interventions
School opinion surveys: • Parents • Staff • Students	• Determining efficacy of programs • Directing senior leadership and board attention • Improvement plans • Strategic plans
Student academic outcomes and destinations after leaving school	• Determining efficacy of programs • Identifying staff needing assistance • Student interventions
• Financial data (common items) • Working capital • Total expenditure per student • Wages as a % of total expenditure • Debt per student • Total recurrent income per student • Outstanding fees per student	• Guiding spending, resourcing and budgets • Funding • Strategic prioritisation
Nationally Consistent Collection of Data (NCCD)	• Educational adjustments made for learning and/or physical difficulties and disabilities • Attracting government funding

Now we know which tests are being dished out, when they are done and what their general purpose is. The next step is to do something meaningful with the data. This means we need to understand what we're looking at. We tend to assume that teachers can always interpret data. Not true! When you do get the hang of it, the data begins to tell a story. It's this story that teachers can do something with. Reading data is like one of those optical illusions where you stare at a page with squiggly lines, trying to see a unicorn or a bear or a starfish. Gradually the image starts to emerge. Suddenly, something previously obscured can be seen. As teachers, we may find reams of data plonked in front of us at a staff meeting. We are given 30 minutes to try and make sense of it and we haven't even been given the keys to unlock the meaning. So we nod politely at each other and at the person who has produced it all, without really knowing what the heck we are looking at.

Table 3 lists types of tests and provides some advice as to how to interpret the results. Table 4 lists the more common ways we might use the data to make decisions around teaching and learning. The interpretation advice provided here is very basic. For further advice around data interpretation, I recommend the work of Selena Fisk (2022).

Understanding assessment and test results

Type of test	Advice
Norm-referenced tests	Norm-referenced tests compare a child's abilities with those of others. These tests are carefully designed using psychometric principles so that performance can be compared to the 'expected' range for children in that age group or year level (often referred to as a reference group).
Criterion-referenced tests	Criterion-referenced tests assess skills or knowledge without comparing a particular child to others. They do not indicate performance in relation to an expected range, but whether a child has achieved certain objectives or met certain criteria.

Type of test	Advice
Percentiles	The percentile rank system (0 to 100) tells you how many children scored equal to or below a particular child on a task or test. If a child's score is at the 18th percentile in a group of 100 students, 18 students would have had the same score or a lower score on the task or test. This also means that 82 of those 100 students would have had a higher score. To interpret percentiles, we use the normal distribution as the base. A percentile rank of 50 is the average. A percentile rank of between 16 and 84 reflects average range. A percentile rank of 20 could be described as low average, and a percentile rank of 80 could be described as high average.
Stanines	This system divides a range of possible test scores into 9 groups called stanines. A stanine score tells you which group a child's score is in, with the lowest score being Stanine 1 and the highest being Stanine 9. Below-average scores fall into Stanines 1, 2 and 3. Average scores fall into Stanines 4, 5 and 6. Above-average scores fall into Stanines 7, 8 and 9.
Standard scores	Standard scores measure a child's test performance against other children of the same age, showing how far above or below the average range a particular score sits. To interpret standard scores, we use normal distribution as the base. A standard score of 100 is the average. A standard score of between 85 and 115 reflects average range. A standard score of 88 could be described as low average, and a standard score of 112 could be describe as high average. Standard scores below 85 reflect a performance that is below the expected range for a student of that age and/or year level. The lower the score, the more difficulty is being experienced by the student.

Methods of Interpretation

In compiling this advice, I acknowledge the work of the Victorian Department of Education.

Method	Advice
Comparing students	Standard testing outcomes cannot definitively indicate learning difficulties. However, a student who consistently scores in the 15th percentile or lower for their year level likely has some form of learning difficulty.
Looking for patterns and trends	If a child's word-reading accuracy exceeds their comprehension when reading out loud and responding to questions, it's possible that:
	They lack necessary oral-language knowledge such as vocabulary, grammatical comprehension and story narrative skills. Oral language, verbal reasoning and listening comprehension may need to be assessed.
	They may have limited background knowledge about the contents of the text.
	They have the oral language needed for comprehension but insufficient automatic word-reading skills.
Identifying learning difficulties	Formal assessment for learning disabilities such as dyslexia must be undertaken by a qualified health professional.
	To identify possible causes of learning difficulty in literacy, start by comparing reading comprehension and word-reading with oral language knowledge and skills, phonological and phonemic knowledge and skills, and metacognition and self-efficacy.
Local vs broad interpretations	There are two ways to interpret literacy assessment outcomes: local or near interpretations and broad-based or far interpretations.
	Local:
	Comparing a child's outcomes on two similar tests or tasks. Inferring where the child is developmentally located in terms of a skill.
	Broad-based:
	Observing and inferring less directly. These interpretations can be drawn from classroom behaviours and triangulation data.

Every school needs to establish its own data map. The staff member responsible for academic life should lead this project, and it's their job to help the rest of the staff to understand the data collected. At the very least you'll know what your school is collecting and why, when it is collected and by whom, and how to interpret the stuff that matters to you and your classes. Finally, the most important piece of the puzzle: you'll have a plan to do something with it.

Three key points from this chapter

1. Data is only worthwhile if you can interpret it and use it to inform your teaching
2. If you don't know why you are collecting certain data, find out whether it's necessary
3. A school needs a data map that spells out what is collected, why it is collected, by whom and for what purpose

PART B

the art of teaching

6

What is this thing called pedagogy?

Here's an interesting experiment: say the word 'pedagogy' out loud to people. Non-teachers usually have no idea what it is. Neither do teachers, more often than not! Most teachers will have at least heard of it and know that it has some connection to the world of teaching and learning. Non-teachers may think it's some medieval torture instrument of the feet or an ancient Greek sculptor.

There are a number of definitions floating around. Here are a few:

- The study of how knowledge and skills are imparted in an educational context (*Encyclopaedia Britannica*, 2006).
- The method and practice of teaching, especially as an academic subject or theoretical concept (*Oxford English Dictionary*, 1991).
- The study of the methods and activities of teaching (*Cambridge Dictionary*, 2013).
- The art and science of teaching students (*Merriam-Webster*, 2022).

I like this last one, the art and science of teaching. Popularised by education researcher Robert Marzano, it's easy to remember and easy to explain to anyone who asks. It captures how teachers bring content to life.

The science of teaching helps us understand how students learn and how content needs to be packaged to connect with every student in a class. The art of teaching is doing this in such a way that every student has the opportunity to connect regardless of context, ability or background. This is the hard bit of teaching. If teaching was as simple as imparting content, classroom teachers would cease to exist. A YouTube clip would do the job, or a teacher on Zoom dishing out content to 100 students. No, the art of teaching is being able to reach a disparate group of young people with all their insecurities, apathy, anxieties and differences. This is why it is so damn hard at times. But when it works, it's magical.

Pedagogy covers much of what we do as teachers. It includes:

- Curriculum to be taught
- Application of instructional methods and tools
- Understanding of learning styles
- Appropriate assessment methods
- Sequential and developmental unit plans
- Provision of useful feedback
- Reporting of progress to parents and caregivers

The term pedagogy comes from the Greek *paidagōgós*, a combination of *paîs* (child) and *agō* (to lead). This word described the slave who would accompany a boy to school, tutor him and impart moral instruction. Pedagogy also brings to mind the relationship between Socrates and Plato, the most influential ancient Greek scholars and arguably the fathers of learning as we know it today. Plato (c. 429–347 BCE) was a student of Socrates (c. 469–399 BCE). The Socratic method of education is an instructional system that uses questions to help students derive meaning. These guys were the architects of the modern student-teacher relationship.

As teachers we sometimes get a little embarrassed or sheepish when we use the word pedagogy. We're reluctant to use it with colleagues in a meeting, and we'd definitely not say it at a dinner party or BBQ with friends. Why is that? Some teachers aren't entirely sure what it means, or in which context to use it. It's not part of their everyday language, so it probably wouldn't pop into their head anyway. The word may come across as a bit pretentious. You might be fully aware of what it means and how to use it, but will choose not to throw it into a conversation. It's part of the Aussie tall poppy syndrome that tells us to not use fancy words when simple ones will suffice. To do so would invite all sorts of eye rolls, something that most teachers try to avoid in a close-knit staffroom. But it's an important word, one that we should know and be proud to say. It sums up our profession, the art and science of teaching. Bloody beautiful, if you ask me! Both the art and the science of teaching can be learned. It will take time, practice, willingness to accept feedback and desire to learn the craft.

Plenty of schools develop their own pedagogical framework. What is that? It's the way in which a school will articulate its methodology of delivering the curriculum, assessing student performance and reporting to parents. It allows a school to tell its staff, students, parents and broader community how it believes effective teaching and learning are best achieved and how it will go about it. It's an important document to have, and something that I look for in a school. It tells me that the staff have talked about pedagogy, done some research, had a good think about it collectively and put something together to pursue it. Dishing out content is the easy part, bringing it to life for all students is the hard part.

This is why a pedagogical framework is important. It's not just some cute marketing ploy that sits on the school website and tries to tell anyone who cares that 'we know teaching'! Sometimes a school will call their pedagogical framework a curriculum framework or a teaching and learning framework. They'll often do this because they want to avoid the word pedagogy or to make the document more accessible to the school and community. Let's not shy away from talking about pedagogy. It's something we should be able to proudly explain.

Teaching is a complex set of skills, characteristics and dispositions. Not everyone can do it, or at least do it well. You need to understand human psychology. You need to gain and maintain the attention of 20 or 30 kids in a class. You need to have the resilience and grit of a rhinoceros. You need to not only know a huge breadth of content, but also how to adjust and amend it so that kids of all ability levels can access it. You need to have the IT and creative skills to design courses of work that can sustain the interest of an adolescent brought up on a diet of video games, TikTok and Marvel movies. You need to be able to work individually in isolation but also as a member of several different teams. You need a variety of communication skills, and you need the emotional and physical fitness to get you through a school year. Welcome to the profession!

Three key points from this chapter

1. Pedagogy is the art and science of teaching
2. It is derived from the Ancient Greek word paidagōgós
3. It encompasses content delivery, assessment, reporting and feedback

7

Assessment tasks, criteria and rubrics

If we can't understand this stuff, how can our kids?

Schools have always been an industrial-sized sorting mechanism. Each year a new batch of children enters the school machine and systematically moves through the year levels. Even if a child fails a year, they are still moved along the conveyor belt of mainstream schooling. It's incessant, unrelenting and sometimes brutal. When they make it to Year 7 or 8, they might be sorted into upper and lower maths or English classes. Then they will reach Year 9 or 10 and may have a chance to follow their interests if electives are available. In Years 11 and 12 they will have to choose subjects that put them on the path to a career, tertiary study or vocational training. Once most kids make it to the end of Year 12, the sorting begins anew.

As part of the school sorting mechanism, all children undergo testing or assessment. It starts with something as simple as reciting the alphabet, writing their name, counting from 1 to 10 or recognising shapes. As they get a little older this assessment expands to reading, spelling, writing and numeracy. It then gradually refines along subject lines: geography, history, maths, science, English and so forth. Literacy and numeracy become almost an afterthought and content mastery is emphasised. Not only do the topics and subject area become more specific, but the complexity deepens. It reaches the point where students are producing 1200-word English essays on the concept of fear as depicted in Mary Shelley's *Frankenstein* and 2000-word scientific reports on the pros and cons of the electric car.

From Prep, children are assessed and reported on constantly. Ultimately, this serves the purpose of separating students in preparation for the workforce. To put it simply, society needs white-collar and blue-collar workers. We need people who can fix things and make things, people who can teach, perform, create, clean, repair, manage, follow and lead. Assessment starts to identify the kind of future work to which students might be suited. If they are good at maths, then certain fields of work will lend themselves to success. If they are good at English, they will find other fields to compliment this strength.

The second thing that assessment does is to tell kids very early on what level of intelligence they have. Unfortunately, the type of intelligence assessed is quite narrow. There is no empathy test, no getting-along-with-others test, no building-stuff test or fixing-stuff test. Kids get pigeonholed, and early impressions can stay with them for the rest of their lives. I implore soon-to-be and current teachers to look at other ways to assess or at least identify and celebrate other types of intelligence. If you want to know what these are, Howard Gardner (1983) has plenty to say about it. This is easy enough to do in the lower years of schooling, but by Years 11 and 12 the assessment is prescribed and we have little—if any—wriggle room.

Assessment gives kids an indication of how well they are travelling in a subject, and hopefully what they can do about it. Feedback on performance in an assessment piece is key to improvement. By feedback I don't simply mean the mark, the grade or the result. I mean useful tips, guided instruction, things to think about next time, suggested alternatives, things they could or should have included, things they got wrong and things they did really well. And don't be ambiguous or wishy-washy with your feedback. Telling a 14-year-old boy that his work needs to be *more thorough* or *more rigorous*, or that he needs to *work harder* means nothing. Be specific, be useful, give examples, provide a model response yourself. You get paid to teach; this is teaching, so get to it. There is no getting around the fact that we have to grade students at the end of term, so we may as well make it meaningful to the kids and their parents. The product is less important than the process.

There are numerous ways to conduct assessment: exams, essays, projects, oral presentations and so forth. These fit into three broad categories known as formative, summative and diagnostic. Another name for formative is informal. Another name for summative is formal. Clear as mud?

Summative is what gets reported on. It's the final grade for a piece of assessment or a unit of work. Formative is unlikely to get reported on. It's the progress mark or the journey towards the final piece of assessment or the grade. It could be a simple quiz or activity. The result of a formative piece is given to the student and sometimes the parent. However, it usually doesn't contribute to the final grade. There may be several smaller pieces of formative assessment combined to provide the summative result. It can be a great opportunity to inform the student of their progress and to point them in the right direction.

A diagnostic assessment is usually a written test, although sometimes it could be verbal. The result may or may not be shared with the child or the parent. It is used for internal purposes by a teacher, a team of teachers, specialist staff or school administrators. Think of how a mechanic will run a diagnostic text of your car when you first bring it in. Or when you see the dentist for the first time in 12 months. You'll hear about what's going wrong and get a plan to fix it.

One of the great mysteries of an assessment piece is often found on the last page, in a matrix or tabular format known as the criteria or rubric. This is what determines an outcome.

Before we go any further, let's recap the key terminology of assessment:

- **Criteria:** a little description or label of what is to be assessed. Each criterion has a title like Knowledge, Application or Evaluation. For some assessment pieces there are three or more criteria. There are typically five standards per criterion, from A through to E, to determine the quality of the work.

- **Rubric:** the whole set of criteria. The rubric is a grid-like framework that visually displays the criteria and standards across one or two pages. Think of it as a bird's-eye view of the entire assessment marking scheme.

- **Objective:** usually used in the context of a learning objective, which will be articulated at the start of a unit of work. It spells out what the teacher is hoping the students will achieve by the end of the unit. The assessment piece should align with this. Watch out: some educators use the phrase 'assessment objective' when referring to criteria.

- **Standard:** the level of difficulty, complexity or quality of the assessment task. It helps a teacher and student determine the result, from an A standard through an E standard. Also called an achievement standard.

- **Weightings:** assessment pieces with more than one criterion may have different levels of marks assigned to them. The total weighting for a unit of assessment will add up to 100 per cent. For instance, a simple content knowledge criterion may be worth 10 per cent while the ability to analyse or evaluate something may be worth well over 50 per cent.

- **Unit of work:** the same as a course of work. It involves medium-term planning, typically over several weeks and multiple lessons, with a defined culminating piece of assessment.

Criteria are often divided to address specific segments of the assessment task. We can thank our old friend Benjamin Bloom (1984) for this (see Chapter 3). There may be one set of criteria for 'Knowledge', another for 'Application' and another for 'Evaluation'. These will differ depending on the subject. Each criterion will be awarded an individual grade, with all individual grades combined to give an overall grade for that piece of assessment. Some assessment tasks are very simple and will be developed to assess only one criterion. Other tasks may be more complex with multiple criteria to assess higher-order thinking. A simple test may ask the child to name the capital cities of 10 given countries. These memorisation tests are useful to a point, but cannot assess a child's ability to take that knowledge and apply it to another situation or problem. A more complex piece of assessment may require the child to write a short story. Here there will be a criterion and grade for spelling and punctuation. There will be a separate criterion for the conventions of a short story including paragraph structures, paragraph linking, and a clear introduction and conclusion. An additional criterion will assess the writer's ability to capture the reader's attention, weave a compelling narrative, build suspense and expose an unexpected twist at the end. A student could achieve an A for spelling, a C for their ability to follow the conventions of a short story, and a D for their ability to sustain a common thread from start to finish. This adds up to a C to C+ result, assuming that all criteria are weighted the same.

Our goal as teachers is to develop the ability of our students to apply their knowledge to different contexts. Memorisation is useful and general knowledge is important, but if those skills cannot be transferred then your kids are disadvantaged. Luckily, we have instructional tools that can be used for a variety of purposes. Direct instruction is very useful for content delivery and knowledge acquisition, but not so good at allowing students the time and space to apply knowledge to different situations. A case study, on the other hand, is perfect for this purpose. If you have a piece of assessment coming up, are you giving your kids the skills and tools to be able to achieve success? If you do direct instruction for eight weeks and the Week 10 assessment requires a great deal of analysis, then cramming this into their heads in Week 9 isn't going to cut it.

Again, it comes back to your planning. Identify the assessment, content and skills needed for success, then embed accordingly throughout the unit. You also need to model an ideal response, and they need to practice before the assessment. Assessment should not be designed to catch them out. It should allow them to test their acquisition of content knowledge and their ability to apply it. Once an assessment piece is graded, you'll report on it to the parents. The end-of-semester report card should not be a surprise. I repeat, it should not be a surprise! If you are failing a kid who would normally be expected to pass, their parents should not learn about it when the semester has ended.

It is your responsibility to explain the criteria to your students before they are assessed. Do it in such a way that they all understand what it will take for them to receive an A. For the love of all things pure and good in this world, if you do not do this for your kids then please do us all a favour and go and lay bricks for a living! Once the assessment is marked, you'll need to be able to intelligently explain to a student why they received a B instead of an A. Imagine playing a game of sport and finishing the game not knowing who won or lost or how many points were scored, or even how to score a point, simply because no one told you how it all worked. The words used in some criteria are quite sophisticated and the phrases used to differentiate an A from a B are subtle, so you need to think carefully as to how you will explain this.

Opinion–writing rubric

Criteria	4	3	2	1
Introduction	Writer includes an effective introduction to their topic.	Writer includes an adequate introduction of their topic.	Introduction of topic is weak.	Writer does not provide a clear introduction.
Opinion Statement	Writer clearly states their opinion on the topic.	Writer adequately states their opinion on the topic.	Writer's opinion is unclear.	Writer does not state their opinion.
Organisation	Writer has a clear organisational structure in which related ideas are grouped together.	Writer has an adequate organisational structure in which related ideas are grouped together.	Organisational structure is confusing and related ideas may or may not be grouped together.	Writer does not provide a clear organisational structure, and supporting ideas are not grouped together.
Linking Words & Phrases	Writer has effectively used a variety of linking words and phrases to connect their opinion and reasons.	Writer has adequately used a variety of linking words and phrases to connect their opinion and reasons.	Writer has included some linking words and phrases, but with little variety to connect their opinion and reasons.	Writer has few to no linking words and phrases to connect their opinion and reasons.
Reasons & Details	Writer provides effective reasons to support opinion and gives supporting details.	Writer provides adequate reasons to support opinion and gives some supporting details.	Writer provides minimal reasons to support opinion and few supporting details.	Writer provides insufficient reason to support details and few or no supporting details.
Conclusion	Writer includes an effective conclusion that relates to their opinion.	Writer includes and adequate conclusion that relates to their opinion.	Conclusion is present but is weak and may or may not relate to their opinion.	Writer does not provide a conclusion, or the conclusion does not connect to their opinion.
Conventions	Writer has few if any errors in grammar, spelling, capitalisation and punctuation.	Writer has some errors in grammar, spelling, capitalisation and punctuation.	Writer has many errors in grammar, spelling, capitalisation and punctuation.	Grammatical, spelling, capitalisation and/or punctuation errors interfere with meaning.

This rubric follows a four-point scale where a 4 is equal to an A, a 3 to a B and so forth. Students are clearly trying to avoid a 1. There are several criteria down the left-hand side of the rubric. Look at the words that differentiate a 4 from a 3. For a 4, words such as *clearly* and *effectively* are used. For a 3, we see *adequate* and *adequately*. This is fine as long as the teacher explains the difference. For instance, can you explain what separates an effective introduction from an adequate introduction? As an adult with substantial experience in the field, even I can't say for certain what this may look like. What chance will a 13-year-old have? What I need is someone to give me some examples and unpack them with me. As a teacher, you must always provide examples of expected responses for each standard of the criteria so your students can see exactly what is required of them. Remember, no surprises and no ambiguity.

Science task rubric

Criteria	0 Incorrect	1 Awareness	2 Definition	3 Limited	4 Extended	5 Comprehensive
Common content knowledge	Provides an incorrect answer without acknowledging the content or with limited understanding of the content.	Does not acknowledge content or has limited understanding.	Emphasises terms, provides a definition-type answer or gives an example that is a representation.	Gives a brief response that has limited detail or elaborates on an example.	Extends the discussion of content to include details that address some components of the content.	Elaborates on the content in a way that presents the complexity of the content area (e.g. connections are made within the concepts emphasised).
Specialised content knowledge	Provides an incorrect answer without acknowledging the content or with limited understanding of the content.	Acknowledges that there is an error but does not understand where the error occurs or why it exists.	Recognises the error and can discuss and relate it to a definition or a procedure. Discussion may be general.	Provides a simple explanation for the error beyond a definition or a procedure. Recognises in general what students get wrong.	Explains the error demonstrated by students. Discussion takes into account the content taught and obstacles in learning the content.	Elaborates on the error demonstrated by students. Contemplates the different problems students may have with the content. Clearly connects the error to the content.
Progressional content knowledge	Provides an incorrect answer without acknowledging the content or with limited understanding of the content.	Acknowledges with uncertainty that there are areas before or after the topic. May mention these topics. Responses are general and contemplative.	Discusses a textbook (curricular) level of understanding. Does not know overarching ideas, but can suggest topics or examples before or after content.	Provides broad topics/ examples before or after content. The topics are often connected to the curriculum. Does not address overarching ideas, but knows the importance of the content.	Explains the placement of the content and can justify the placement. Can identify some overarching ideas.	Elaborates on the content before and after topic. Knows why the content fits where it does and why it is important. Can identify overarching ideas associated with the content area.

Assessment tasks, criteria and rubrics   71

This one starts with the lowest mark first and then progresses up. It has six standards across three criteria or objectives. Have a look at the key words that separate a 5 from a 4. To get a 5 you'll need to *elaborate* a lot, to get a 4 you'll need to *extend* without elaboration. If a teacher doesn't thoroughly explain the difference between elaboration and extension using examples, then how can we ever expect the kids to understand? These are complex terms for a young person. Not only that, but they are written within the context of a subject. This gives them another layer of complexity and specificity.

We are fortunate in Australia to have a national curriculum that uses the same terminology and structures across all subject areas. There are some variations, largely due to the differing natures of subjects, but there are consistencies across the core structures and features. Subject areas are called learning areas. We educators love to confuse the hell out of people, which is ironic considering our line of work! Anyway, the learning areas are Maths, English, Science, Humanities, Arts, Technologies, Health and PE, and Languages. Each learning area from Prep to Year 10 has level descriptors, content descriptors and achievement standards. The latter provide an outline of expected responses for kids at that age or level. Schools should ideally provide a five-point scale (e.g. from A to E) that expands the achievement standards into a rubric to allow teachers to award a mark or a result.

What happens, however, is that all sorts of terminology are being used across the country: exceeding expectations, meeting expectations, working towards expectations, does not meet expectations. Or very high, high, sound, developing, emerging. Or working towards, working at, working beyond. This is only a problem if kids are changing schools regularly. Essentially it all means the same thing, and the same recommendations apply. Explain the criteria, explain the words, show examples, give clear feedback on how to improve, and allow kids to understand why they got a certain mark and what they can do to get better.

Now have a look at the criteria for the subjects of the International Baccalaureate for an alternative point of view.

International Baccalaureate criteria

Subject area	A	B	C	D
Arts	Knowing & understanding	Developing skills	Thinking creatively	Responding
Design	Inquiring & analysing	Developing ideas	Creating the solution	Evaluating
Individuals & Societies	Knowing & understanding	Investigating	Communicating	Thinking critically
Language Acquisition	Listening	Reading	Speaking	Writing
Language & Literature	Analysing	Organising	Producing text	Using language
Mathematics	Knowing & understanding	Investigating patterns	Communicating	Applying mathematics in real-life contexts
Physical Health & Education	Knowing & understanding	Planning for performance	Applying and performing	Reflecting and improving performance
Sciences	Knowing & understanding	Inquiring and designing	Processing and evaluating	Reflecting on the impacts of science
Personal Project	Planning	Applying skills	Reflecting	

Assessment tasks for the International Baccalaureate (IB) are assessed according to only four criteria across all subjects. However, these criteria are quite different across subjects. You can see that for most subjects there is an increasing complexity of criteria.

Whatever the words used and however the assessment is structured, it comes down to your ability to make sense of it and intelligently explain it to students and parents.

> **Three key points from this chapter**
>
> 1. If you can't understand and explain the criteria, what hope do your kids have?
> 2. Assessment should not be a surprise: prepare for it, plan for it, model it
> 3. Know the purposes of formative, summative and diagnostic assessments

8

Teaching kids on the spectrum

Let's start with a note on language: how you speak about autism is an important issue to many. Autism spectrum disorder (ASD) and autism are the same thing. Autism is a lifelong neurodevelopmental disorder. Some autistic people and their families prefer to talk about autism without emphasis on the disorder. Some prefer a person-first approach: 'student with autism' or 'child with autism'. Others may prefer identity-first language: 'autistic student' rather than a 'student with autism'. Personally, I try to use the phrase 'student with autism'.

In compiling this chapter, I must acknowledge the work of Autism Spectrum Australia (Aspect). I highly recommend this wonderful organisation for anyone wishing to explore this topic further. I'd also advise you to check out the work of Tony Attwood, a prominent ASD educator and researcher and a great source of advice. I've added some of his work to the reference section of this book.

You may have heard the terms *neurodivergent* and *neurotypical* and scratched your head wondering whether yet another phrase had been invented to describe autism. A neurotypical person is an individual who thinks and behaves in ways that are considered standard by the general population. Neurodivergence and neurodiversity are umbrella terms that capture all the largely cognitive differences across the rich tapestry of humanity, including ASD and conditions such as ADHD and dyslexia.

Plenty of teachers think of autism as a linear continuum. They may picture a student sitting along this line from mild to severe, minor to major. This is simply not correct. Look, it's an easy way to view the autistic world and to categorise a kid with autism. It allows us to better understand autism, to explain it and to cater for it. As teachers we see kids all the time who have mild autistic traits or characteristics, right through to a non-verbal child with profound autistic traits or characteristics. To place these kids on a continuum from mild to extreme is very common practice. It was in fact the main way that kids with autism were originally 'classified'. It's not only an instinctive reaction for a teacher, but also a historical artefact of what we all once did.

Think instead of autism as a circle or spectrum. There are a variety of physical, social and emotional characteristics that we all possess as humans. Every single one of us is more attuned to or adept at certain things. Some of us are more social, some have more emotional intelligence, some have better hand-eye coordination. Some can more easily communicate with a variety of audiences, and some enjoy crowds while others could think of nothing worse. We all experience these traits and characteristics to varying degrees. Kids with autism simply sit at the outer edge of intensity for some of these. Autism may affect their communication, motor skills, social skills, sensory perception, language skills, executive functioning, interests and routines.

I'd like to share some questions about autism that I'm often asked or hear discussed in staff rooms, parent groups and my own friendship groups.

What is the definition of autism?

Autism is a developmental disability significantly affecting verbal and non-verbal communication and social interaction. It is a lifelong, nonprogressive neurological disorder that typically appears before the age of three years (Price, 2022).

Autism refers to a broad range of conditions characterised by challenges with social skills, repetitive behaviours, speech and nonverbal communication (Beardon, 2019).

Autism is a developmental disability caused by differences in the brain. People with ASD may behave, communicate, interact and learn in ways that are different from most other people (Hewitson, 2018).

What are some possible signs of autism in children and teenagers?

- Reluctance to make eye contact
- Communication styles ranging from limited speech to highly developed vocabularies
- Seeming to prefer playing alone or appearing to be in their own world
- Intense attachments to certain subjects, activities or interests
- Struggling in interactions with other children
- Speech dominated by their favourite topics
- Talking in a monotonous tone and using unusual expressions or accents
- Talking 'at' others rather than having a two-way conversation; not good at 'small talk'
- Difficulty interpreting and using facial expressions and gestures
- Being less aware of socially expected behaviour (e.g. criticising the teacher or refusing to join a classroom activity)
- Being easily overwhelmed in social situations and needing time alone
- Not enjoying situations that most children like (e.g. school excursions)
- Trouble with co-operative play; wanting to play the same way every time
- Having no or few friends
- Displaying unusual physical movements such as touching, biting, rocking or finger flicking
- Having a strong need to follow rules and routines, and becoming upset when these change
- Being over- or under-sensitive to sensory stimuli (e.g. textures, sounds, smells, tastes)
- Sometimes displaying aggressive behaviour to avoid stressful situations
- Anxiety

Differences typically experienced by children with autism

- **Initiations and responses during communication.** Some students might have sophisticated language skills, and others might use few to no words. Autistic students tend to speak very honestly, and may misunderstand others when language isn't direct (e.g. sarcasm or jokes). They may take longer to understand communication, and some will make statements that don't fit the flow of conversation or context.

- **Interpretations and use of nonverbal communication.** Autistic students may avoid or dislike eye contact. Their facial expressions may be less expressive than those of other students. They may be less likely to use gestures (e.g. pointing) when communicating. Students may become frustrated and distressed when their attempts to communicate verbally or nonverbally are misunderstood, which can result in challenging behaviours. Don't insist that a child with autism look at you when you're giving an instruction.

- **Interactions and understanding in social contexts.** Students with autism may misunderstand social interactions, including unspoken social conventions such as taking turns. These social difficulties mean that they can end up playing alone. They are often keen to join in, but just might not know how. Other students may become frustrated with their apparent inability to 'get it', which can add to their social exclusion.

- **Behaviours or interests.** Students with autism tend to like doing things in a particular way or order. This often means that they follow routines and class rules well. They may have a favourite activity that they are happy to do over and over again, and they may need warning before the class switches between tasks. They can focus intensely on a specific interest for extended periods of time.

- **Reactions to sensory input.** Some students may be discomforted by loud noises or particular sounds or textures. As every student with autism is different, it is important for teachers to understand the student's sensory needs. They can then provide appropriate supports and ensure that the classroom environment is inclusive.

When did autism 'emerge'?

Because autism has become so much more prevalent in recent years, you might think of it as a new phenomenon. But it's actually been discussed for more than 100 years—and our thinking about the condition has changed dramatically during that time. Here are key events in autism history:

- **1908:** The word *autism* is used to describe a subset of withdrawn and self-absorbed schizophrenic patients.
- **1943:** Austrian-American child psychiatrist Leo Kanner publishes a paper describing 11 children who were highly intelligent but displayed 'a powerful desire for aloneness' and 'an obsessive insistence on persistent sameness.' He later names their condition 'early infantile autism.'
- **1944:** Austrian psychiatrist Hans Asperger describes a 'milder' form of autism that came to be known as Asperger's syndrome. The cases he reported were all boys who were highly intelligent but had specific obsessive interests and trouble with social interactions.
- **1967:** Austrian-American psychologist Bruno Bettelheim popularises a theory that 'refrigerator mothers' caused autism by not loving their children enough. (Spoiler alert: this is completely false.) Autism is also classified under schizophrenia in the *International Statistical Classification of Diseases and Related Health Problems*, although we now know there is no link between the conditions.
- **1977:** Research on twins finds that autism is largely caused by genetics and biological differences in brain development.
- **1980:** 'Infantile autism' is listed in the *Diagnostic and Statistical Manual of Mental Disorders* (DSM) for the first time; the condition is also officially separated from childhood schizophrenia.
- **1987:** The DSM replaces 'infantile autism' with a more expansive definition of 'autism disorder', and includes a checklist of diagnostic criteria. Norwegian-American psychologist Ivar Lovaas publishes the first study that demonstrates how intensive behaviour therapy can help children with autism.
- **1991:** Schools begin identifying children on the spectrum and offering them support.

- **1994:** Asperger's syndrome is added to the DSM, expanding the autism spectrum to include milder cases in which individuals tend to be more highly functioning.
- **1998:** A study published in *The Lancet* suggests that the measles-mumps-rubella (MMR) vaccine causes autism. This finding is quickly debunked.
- **2000:** Despite any link to autism having been debunked, vaccine manufacturers remove thimerosal (a mercury-based preservative) from all routinely given childhood vaccines due to continuing public fears about its role in autism.
- **2009:** The US Centers for Disease Control and Prevention (CDC) estimates that 1 in 110 children have autism spectrum disorders, up from 1 in 150 in 2007, noting that the increase stems at least in part from improved screening and diagnostic techniques.
- **2013:** The DSM-5 folds all subcategories of autism into one umbrella diagnosis of autism spectrum disorder (ASD). Asperger's syndrome is no longer considered a separate condition. ASD is defined by two categories: 1) Impaired social communication and/or interaction. 2) Restricted and/or repetitive behaviours.

(SOURCES: ATTWOOD, 2009; ASPECT AUSTRALIA, 2023; BEARDON, 2019.)

Has autism increased in recent decades?

Diagnosis has increased, but autism has not. Contrary to conspiracy theories, it is not caused by environmental factors such as vaccines, helicopter parents, crop spraying or preservatives in food. There is, however, some evidence that the rate is increasing because of the rising age of parents, especially fathers.

I believe that the rise in autism diagnoses is largely social, not biological. It's not that more children are developing symptoms of autism, but rather that multifaceted social, educational, medical and political factors are increasing the rates of diagnosis and changing the way in which autism is now classified.

Can someone 'catch' autism like a virus?

You can't catch autism. Some people are nervous about allowing their children to come into contact with autistic peers out of anxiety over contagion. Autism can't be passed from person to person through any means other than heredity.

What is the cause of autism?

There is no one single cause of autism. Research suggests that it develops from a combination of genetic and environmental influences. These influences appear to increase the likelihood that a child will develop autism. However, it's important to keep in mind that increased risk is not the same as *cause*. For example, some gene changes associated with autism can also be found in people who don't have the disorder. Similarly, not everyone exposed to an environmental risk factor for autism will develop the disorder. In fact, most will not.

Research tells us that autism tends to run in families. The following factors may lead to increased likelihood of autism:

- Advanced parent age (either parent)
- Pregnancy and birth complications such as extreme prematurity, low birth weight, multiple pregnancies (twins, triplets)
- Pregnancies spaced less than one year apart

Can autism be cured?

Autism is a lifelong condition and currently cannot be cured. It can, however, be treated. With the right early intervention, most children experience significant improvement in their quality of life and many learn to function independently in mainstream school.

How is autism diagnosed?

Diagnosis can be difficult because there is no medical test to detect autism. Doctors look at the child's developmental history and behaviour to make a diagnosis.

Autism can sometimes be detected in children of 18 months or younger. The diagnosis of a two-year-old by an experienced professional can be considered reliable. However, some children may not receive a final diagnosis until much later. Many are not diagnosed until adolescence or adulthood, and many are not diagnosed at all. This means that people with autism might not get the early help they need.

Diagnosing children as early as possible is key to ensuring that they receive the services and supports that will allow them to reach their full potential. Commonly the diagnosis will be made by a multidisciplinary team including a paediatrician (or child and adolescent psychiatrist), a psychologist and a speech pathologist. Other health professionals may provide input if required.

Teachers cannot diagnose ASD. The possibility of autism may also be a very sensitive topic to raise with parents. This is how I would advise you to approach it:

Go to your school's learning support or enrichment department, and seek advice from a colleague familiar with the process of diagnosis. If you are the soul charged with the responsibility of approaching the child's parents, talk to them face-to-face with compassion and empathy. Point out the characteristics that you are noticing, highlight the impact of these on their child's learning and wellbeing, and suggest that a formal diagnosis would be ideal. Make sure to take some referral numbers and addresses to give them.

Are there any differences in autism between the sexes?

While autism is more common in boys, we now recognise that autism can get overlooked in girls. This is especially true for girls of 'normal' or high intelligence.

Girls are better at camouflaging or masking their autism by imitating other people when they're socialising. They can also feel more pressure to conform to standards and follow expected behaviours.

Girls with autism may only have one or few close friendships, and will be intense and possessive about those friendships.

What's the difference between high-functioning and low-functioning autism?

High-functioning autism (HFA) is an unofficial term used for people whose autism symptoms appear mild. The official diagnostic term is ASD Level 1. In the past, people who fit the description of HFA would likely have been diagnosed with Asperger's syndrome.

The severity of ASD is often described by a level from 1 to 3, based on support needed:

- **Level 1** requires some support
- **Level 2** requires substantial support
- **Level 3** requires very substantial support

Terms such as 'high-functioning' and 'low-functioning' can be misleading; people with autism who appear to function very well can still need a high level of support.

Australian schools have to collect data on students with disabilities. This includes those who are formally diagnosed with ASD, and those who are not formally diagnosed but are receiving support or adjustments. This exercise is called the Nationally Consistent Collection of Data or NCCD, and is usually done around August. Funding is provided by the federal and state governments based on the number of students affected at each year level.

What is the difference between autism and Asperger's syndrome?

Asperger's syndrome is no longer considered a valid diagnostic classification, and is now known simply as Level 1 ASD. Previously used to describe a form of 'high-functioning' autism (HFA), it was removed from the *Diagnostic and Statistical Manual of Mental Disorders* (DSM) in 2013 when the fifth edition (DSM-5) was published.

Teaching kids with autism

Here are suggestions for teachers who have kids in their class diagnosed with autism or showing traits and characteristics without an official diagnosis. I recommend the program AllPlay, developed by Australian researcher Professor Nicole Rinehart. Again, ASD expert Tony Attwood is a great source of advice. Special education expert Sue Larkey also provides wonderful practical strategies for teachers.

Every child with autism is different, and there is no 'one size fits all'. This means that the characteristics of autism may differ significantly from one student to another.

Consider adjustments to your communication style

- **Provide a clear schedule and routine.** Visual cues and schedules can help students understand what is coming up and when they should complete a transition from one activity to another.
- **Give a warning when a transition is coming up.** Children who find it difficult to move from one activity to another often feel less unsettled if they are warned about the transition (e.g. 'In two minutes we are going to pack away and go to art'). Provide clear instructions about the transition.

Tailor activities to be as inclusive as possible

- **Some tasks may need to be modified for a student** Where you can, use concrete materials (images to supplement text, blocks to model maths) rather than abstract concepts. Where needed, provide simplified text and pictures showing how to complete a task.
- **Where possible, add the child's interests into the learning process.** For example, if a student is motivated by cars, offer a small bundle of toy cars for addition and subtraction. When the student completes their maths, encourage them by giving them some time to play with the cars. A worksheet with cars or a story about cars may also suffice.

Provide positive feedback

- **Give encouragement and correction.** Consider giving positive feedback and correction immediately when children are learning a task or behaviour. This can be reduced gradually as they build their capability.

- **Encourage their interests.** Some children may be highly motivated by their interests. Consider letting a child engage in an activity related to their interests as encouragement for their efforts.

- **Express positive regard and support.** Teacher emotional support and encouragement helps a student with autism achieve better results. Help a child know that they are valued and supported.

- **Students may need to practice a task or behaviour many times.** Lots of time to practice in different settings and with different materials can help students learn to use that skill in other situations.

- **Offer fewer tasks with more opportunities to practice.** This helps children to learn tasks and may be more helpful than offering many tasks with little opportunity to practice.

- **Help them with one-on-one attention.** When a task is new, children will learn best with help (prompts, demonstrations, encouragement). This help can be gradually reduced as they become more capable. Help can be provided by teachers or other students.

Other suggestions

Minimise background noise and distractions while giving instructions. Noise-reducing headphones may help a child if they find the classroom or playground too loud. Support children to learn social behaviours by modelling them yourself. Consider prompting them to use social behaviours, such as asking another child to play, share, or wait their turn. Some children with autism may have much knowledge about a topic if it is one of their special interests, so give them an opportunity to share their knowledge with others. Provide a safe space in the classroom so that children can self-soothe and reset when experiencing challenges.

Three key points from this chapter

1. Autism is also known as Autistic Spectrum Disorder or ASD
2. People with autism aren't simply 'a little bit autistic' or 'very autistic', but have diverse strengths and weaknesses
3. There are three levels of ASD, with Level 1 associated with minor support requirements and Level 3 with substantial support requirements

9

Boys and girls: do they learn differently, and if they do then so what?

The co-ed vs single-sex education debate has been around since mass education began during the time of the Industrial Revolution. It exists to this day and probably will for many years to come. While there is not a definitive 'boy brain' or 'girl brain', there are some differences in brain chemistry, size and structure between the sexes. The work of clinician, researcher and neurologist Frances Jensen spells this out very clearly (see *The Teenage Brain*, 2015). Brain development affects children's learning, their absorption and retention of information, and the ways in which they organise themselves and approach certain tasks. We should have a decent grasp of children's cognitive development and know how to adapt our teaching accordingly.

Since there are some biological differences to the ways their brains are wired, boys and girls may often display certain differences in their learning styles. However, we should be careful not to simplify our teaching according to stereotypes that don't reflect the reality of the children before us. The days of boys being funnelled into trades or a profession and girls being funnelled into nursing, teaching and secretarial jobs are long gone.

Let me get something very clear on this topic: each child learns in a way that is unique to them as an individual human being. All children benefit from a teacher who cares for them, plans well, provides detailed feedback, has structures in place, adapts their delivery style and content, and has high expectations.

I have taught in all-girls, all-boys and co-ed schools across both the public and independent schooling sectors. I have sent my own children to each type of school, and have seen students thrive in all of them. I've seen male and female teachers at a co-ed school teach in a way that is simply magical, resonating with both girls and boys on a very personal level. These teachers have adjusted and adapted to achieve success. Likewise, I have seen some appalling practices by supposed experts in single-sex schools where the students were disengaged, underperforming and generally directionless. What matters most is the skill of the teacher, the leadership of the school, the programs and practices employed by the school, and the overall ambition of the collective school community to push for continual improvement.

My experience, research and hard-earned lessons have taught me that variations, considerations and adjustments can be made to connect with girls and boys alike. Adapting your teaching with these in mind will give your students a greater chance of success and engender them with a love of school. It will also give you a greater sense of fulfilment as their teacher. With this in mind, there are some interesting things to know about male and female brain development that may assist you in the classroom. For further advice on this topic, I have found the work of Louann Brizendine and Abigail Norfleet James particularly helpful. Both experts are referenced at the end of this book.

The boy brain and how it affects learning

Boys in the womb are developing into little testosterone machines: in his first few months, a male baby will produce as much testosterone as an adult man! Levels then plummet until the boy reaches puberty.

Male brains are up to 11 per cent larger than those of females, relative to overall body size difference. This has no impact on brain function.

Males have more connectivity within a brain hemisphere (there are two hemispheres—left and right), and these hemispheres operate more independently of each other than we see in girls. As a result, boys may need to sound out and look at words more than girls do.

Boys tend to perform better in visual and spatial integration. This gives them an advantage in navigation, assembling stuff and hand-eye coordination.

During puberty, testosterone reduces connections between some brain cells and fortifies connections between others. The issue here is that the last part to be bulked up is the pre-frontal cortex responsible for decision-making, problem-solving and impulse control (well, that explains a few things!).

Because the pre-frontal cortex is still developing in teens, the amygdala is asked to step up. The amygdala is tasked with emotions, impulses, and aggression (and this explains a few more things!).

The girl brain and how it affects learning

Girls make some testosterone before they're born, too, but not nearly as much as boys. And while girls do produce the female hormone oestrogen, their brains get less of it than those of boys in the neonatal period.

The region called the caudate that helps control language and emotion tends to be larger in female brains. The language development of girls is up to one-and-half years faster than that of boys in reading and writing.

Part of the larger corpus callosum, which bridges the two brain hemispheres, is larger in female brains. It appears that girls use both sides of their brains to solve problems and are better at switching between tasks.

Girls show superior ability to memorise and recite lists of words, have greater finger dexterity and are better at thinking on the spot.

Infant girls have earlier and more advanced sensory and cognitive development: vision, hearing, memory, smell and touch. They respond more readily to human voices and faces, leading boys in motor and language skills and identifying emotional expressions better. Boys do catch up though.

Girls develop organisational and attention skills faster than boys. Schools, especially in the secondary years, require attention, planning and organisation—which means that girls have a distinct advantage.

The nature vs nurture debate: biology is not destiny

We know that there are physical differences in brain development between boys and girls, and that these affect how they may learn and interact with their environment. But the environment also impacts brain development. Our brains change based on what we are exposed to. If a baby girl is always dressed in pink, given dolls to play with and herded towards more genteel or feminine interests, she is likely to keep following this pattern as she grows up. The same applies to boys with a love of trucks or sport.

There still exist certain stereotypes around what girls and boys are respectively good at. Biological brain development does appear to have some impact, but this is negligible over time. There is no hard evidence to suggest that girls are biologically predisposed to childcare or nursing, or that they are less inclined to excel in maths (Jensen, 2015). We only need to see the increasing number of girls choosing maths and science subjects and pursuing careers in these fields. We must expose our children to all types of cognitive, sensory, social, linguistic and physical experiences to develop their brains, interests, skills and dispositions.

Some teaching approaches and considerations that may assist with boys

Boys are more likely than girls to disengage from school and have poor academic achievement. When we think of disengaged boys we tend to think of the class clown, but this is rarely the case. The disengaged boy is usually not known for behavioural problems. Instead he is uninterested, often unprepared, and gives up easily. His 'care factor' is zero.

So how do we reach disengaged boys?

- **Reward effort.** Find ways to recognise and celebrate it. Boys may perceive intelligence as fixed, but effort is in their control. It must be encouraged.
- **Relationships are king with boys.** They want to know that they are liked by their teacher. They need boundaries. Be friendly, fair and fun.
- **Connect through action.** Most boys learn by doing, so find ways to include experiential learning experiences. Use games and competitions, real-life stories and examples. Embrace technology. You must make lessons interesting and a little fun, with some variety. Technology is one way to do this.
- **A sense of freedom.** Give them plenty of opportunity to move around the room or space. Give them some choice in content, pace and assessment.
- **The rule of 3.** Place a limit of three on class rules or task instructions. Anything more than that and things get forgotten (the same applies to adults, by the way!).

Some teaching approaches and considerations that may assist with girls

Girls are no different to boys when it comes to the benefits of establishing a relationship. Who would have known! If a girl can see that you like and respect her, you're off to a good start.

What should you consider when teaching girls?

- **Girls love group work and peer-to-peer teaching.** You will need to oversee the group allocations and dynamics, as girls can be vicious within groups at times. Remember that you manage the classroom dynamics. Don't let them dictate class seating arrangements all the time. Move them around.
- **Talk, think, do.** Girls succeed when they are given a problem, can talk about it and then reflect on what was discussed before getting into it. Use collaboration, interaction and involvement but also give them time and space to dig into a task or project independently.

- ***If I sit here quietly, no will notice me.*** Keep an eye on the quiet girls. They may be struggling academically or socially, so they'll try to hide it and can easily slip under the radar in a busy classroom. Beware also the perfectionist. Encourage a have-a-go attitude to help overcome anxiety and the desire to always get it right.
- **Girls love structure.** They want to know what is ahead of them and respond to praise, reassurance and confidence-building. Give them what you may consider typical boy stuff to do: hands-on learning, technology, movement.

If you are looking for a bit more advice on this topic, explore the work of Andrew Fuller, Michael Gurian and Maggie Hamilton.

Boys will work for schools that work for boys

As I have done significantly more work with boys throughout my career, I feel that I can talk a bit more intelligently on this topic. Here is some advice for those of you who find yourselves teaching boys, particularly of the teenage variety.

Where normal boy activity and developmental levels are accommodated, 'boy problems' dissipate. Boys will exhibit high levels of self-control and discipline in an environment that allows them the freedom to be active. They learn by doing and thrive on relationships built through group activities, camps and projects.

Meet their basic needs for love, care and respect. The presence of kind, decent, honourable men has a tremendously calming effect. Each boy needs a mentor who is sensitive and can relate to his personality and interests. Violence and hostility are not the result of testosterone. Don't buy into that myth. Encourage the nurturing, caring emotional life of a boy.

Build their emotional literacy and offer an alternative to the Boy Code that rewards invulnerability and aggression. Supervise those areas where the Boy Code operates most forcibly: the bus, PE, the playground, lining up for class or the tuckshop.

Monitor the social wellness of the boy. We all need friends, and boys who do not have friends or find it hard to make and retain friends will find less wholesome avenues for this connection. Become sensitive to the early signs of mask- or code-weariness: drugs, isolation, acting out or violence.

Never shame them in front of their peers. If they require some level of learning support, make it subtle. Where a boy's experience of belonging is greater than his sense of difference, then the shame, inadequacy and anger will drop away and he will learn.

They will respond to all opportunities—sport, music, drama, debating—when the school encourages and supports this. Anticipate significant changes in the life of a boy: year-level changes, school changes, athletics trials, camps, family trauma. Plan for these events and provide support. Create a partnership between boy, parents and school. Don't wait to call only when a negative issue arises.

Five ways that schools can fail boys

1. Ignoring below-par reading and writing, thereby decreasing self-esteem and interest in learning
2. Not understanding the social and emotional needs of boys or handling those needs poorly
3. Not understanding the Boy Code of tough masculinity
4. Curricula and teaching methods that are not particularly boy-friendly
5. A lack of mentors, particularly male mentors

The Boy Code

Learn the Boy Code not to reinforce it but to understand why some boys act a certain way.

What does the Boy Code demand of a boy? Show only your action-oriented heroic self, it says. Express anger, but supress all other emotions. Cover up your gentle, caring side. Do not be vulnerable, do not cry or act scared. Suppress feelings of rejection and loss. Try to look cool and in control. Hide feelings of insecurity by being the class clown. Reject threats or shaming by being dismissive and aloof. Do not engage in topics of conversation beyond the weather, girls or sport. It's okay to brag as a way to hide a lack of confidence. Don't appear as too smart or eager to do well academically. Feel free to belittle any boy who breaches the code.

The Boy Code is a mask, and it's important that we role-model a different way of being that helps gradually remove the mask.

Three key points from this chapter

1. There are differences in boy and girl brains throughout childhood and adolescence that affect learning, so adjust your teaching accordingly
2. Girls respond to 'talk, think, do' while boys respond to 'friendly, fair, fun'
3. All students respond well to a teacher who cares, plans well and provides helpful feedback

10

Feedback: how and when to give it

If we aren't giving feedback to students, how do we expect them to improve and learn? Your job is to deliver content to a child in a way that makes sense to their own unique way of absorbing information. The child will demonstrate what they have learned by producing work to be assessed. You then judge them on their ability to regurgitate the content via whatever medium you have chosen. The result of your judgment is what sorts them for the future world of work.

Your other job as a teacher is to provide advice to the child along this journey. This advice should improve their acquisition of knowledge and skills that let them function in the world, and it should help them achieve results that will broaden their opportunities. That is the purpose of feedback. There is substantial evidence to indicate that constructive and sensitive feedback can accelerate the pace of learning by 50 per cent or an additional 6 months or more over a year (Dylan Wiliam, 2017). If this isn't reason enough to invest a bit of time into getting this feedback thing sorted, then I give up. Feedback done right is a game-changer.

There are right and wrong ways to provide feedback. The wrong way is to be nebulous, ambiguous, wishy-washy. There's no point in saying 'develop this further' or 'this needs more clarity' without detail or examples. Even worse is underlining or circling an apparent error or weakness without explanation. The wrong way is to only find fault in what your students do. There must be something good that you can congratulate them on before delving into what they can improve. We need to build kids up and give them the confidence to take healthy risks, to have a go. The wrong way is to criticise a student's intelligence or give them the impression that no matter how hard they try they'll never attain an improved outcome.

The right way begins with establishing a healthy classroom culture of feedback, and ideally one that permeates the whole school. How is this achieved, I hear you ask?

- Be constructive, not negative
- Be positive and encouraging
- Welcome feedback yourself and demonstrate this as a teacher
- Encourage healthy risks and a have-a-go mentality
- Encourage students to support each other

All staff should do these things, including the senior leadership of the school.

The next thing is to work out how you will structure feedback. This gives kids some signposts to look for. There are a few models available, but essentially it looks like this:

- Where am I going?
- Am I on track?
- What do I need to do next?

What does this mean in a practical sense? If a student of mine were to receive feedback on an analysis of the concept of fear as depicted in Mary Shelley's *Frankenstein*, it could look like this:

> *Well done Abdul on getting your draft in on time. You have made a solid effort and with some work between now and the final due date, we'll see improvement. These are the areas that you need to work on:*

- *I can see that you are trying to explain how fear is man-made. You need to explore this concept further by using examples such as how 'the monster' was treated and how this treatment nurtured a growing sense of anger and resentment.*
- *You could explain further how the rejection by Victor contributed to the monster's feeling of betrayal.*
- *Your introduction does not establish the purpose of the analysis. Some paragraphs are simply descriptions of the text rather than analysis, but this can be addressed.*
- *Far too many grammatical errors, so clean those up.*

You have two weeks between now and the due date. Work on these things and if you have any questions come and speak with me. Good luck.

Correction is not feedback

There is a difference between correction and feedback. Correction is what you do when you fix up spelling errors, punctuation, the flow of a sentence or paragraph, the structure or format of a report. I make corrections all the time. No point in allowing a kid to continue to spell something incorrectly. Fix it for them or show them how to spell it correctly. We can't let our kids continue to mix up there, *their* and *they're,* or to completely mess up the whole *i before e except after c* rule. Basic stuff like that can be rectified quickly. Sometimes I'll just circle something. Because I have prepped my kids for this, they will know that a circle indicates an error and understand that it's up to them to get it right with a bit of their own investigation. Feedback is something much more broad, expansive and instructive than this type of correction.

If you don't remember anything else from this chapter, at least try to remember this. Feedback needs to be:

- Frequent—not delayed or infrequent
- Constructive—not negative or condescending
- Instructive—not vague or shallow

Because I like to give practical examples, here are some feedback stems that you can use:

I think you did a great job when you [insert specifics]. It showed that you had…

I would love to see you do more of X as it relates to Y…

I really think you have a superpower around X…

I think that you should do more of…. and less of…

You need to do more research around…

You will benefit by restructuring…

Sometimes a feedback form may assist you. A form like this allows you to provide consistency and ensure some level of equity. If used across an entire school it will provide consistency and familiarity across classes and year levels. Pretty powerful stuff!

Sample student feedback form

Name:

Class:

Date:

Project / task / assessment title:

Quality of work	Yes / no
Am I on track?	
What qualities does this work demonstrate?	
How does this work demonstrate the goal of the project?	
What is missing from this work?	
How does this work compare with that of others?	
What do I need to do next?	
Guiding feedback criteria	
Feedback is focused on the project	

Quality of work	Yes / no
Feedback is simple	
Feedback is do-able	
Feedback helps the work become better	
Feedback is specific and detailed	

Three key points from this chapter

1. Correction is not feedback
2. Feedback is frequent, constructive and instructive
3. Feedback structure: where am I going, am I on track, what do I need to do next?

PART C
the practicalities of teaching

11

Classroom management 101

Behaviour management is how you deal with poor conduct when it occurs. Classroom management is how you prevent poor conduct from occurring, or at least mitigate it. One is reactive, the other is proactive.

Classroom management is firmly entrenched in Chapter 2. It starts with thinking about how you want to reduce disruption and enhance learning. Managing your classroom begins before the students even enter the room. In fact, it begins well before they line up outside the room. You should incorporate it when you start to plan your unit, which may be months in advance. Prior planning prevents poor performance—this applies to classroom management. When you plan for the management of your class, your lessons and your individual students, start by thinking about how you use your physical space. The layout of the room, the walls, the furniture. You need to consider these fixtures as tools.

Then you need to think about desk positions. There is nothing wrong with getting the desk layout exactly as you want it before the kids walk in. Spend five minutes organising this and it will save you time and grief. Then think about where specific students sit and who they sit next to. For some classes you'll need very deliberate seating arrangements. The kids can sit where they want after they've shown you that they can be responsible, self-regulated independent learners. Sure, there can be co-design: some input, some collaboration, some personal choice. But if that personal choice comes at the expense of learning and hampers your ability to teach effectively, then you need to make changes.

At the start of each lesson, take five minutes to do these three things:

1. Get the attention of the class
2. Link the current lesson to the previous lesson
3. Tell them what is happening this lesson

Then you get into the body of your lesson. You might have planned this to be teacher-led or based around student project work. Your voice is your greatest teaching tool. Learn to use it accordingly. If you start the lesson at high volume, you'll have nowhere to go when things are unravelling and need reigning in. The kids will become desensitised to your volume.

Plan what you want to achieve and how you will do this: resources, transitions, group work and so forth. If you are using technology, make sure it works and is ready to go. Test it in advance if possible. There is nothing worse than having 30 Year 8 students waiting for you to sort out the data projector because you don't have the right plug, cord or cable. If you've ever wondered what anarchy feels like, welcome to the show!

Be active and proactive within the classroom. Move about the room instead of sitting at your desk the whole lesson. Teaching is not a desk-bound job: it's personal and it's active. Walk around the desks. Check student work. Ask questions to check their understanding. Moving about like this allows you to see whether the kids are on track and paying attention. If a kid is a bit off-task, they won't be for long once they know you'll soon be walking behind them.

If a kid is being a distraction, warn them once or twice then deal with it if it happens a third time. You can do this by moving either the student or whatever is distracting them to another place in the room or outside it altogether. Managing poor behaviour requires a plan, consistency, fairness and a refusal to play favourites. Don't hold a grudge against a kid if they do misbehave. Give them a chance to improve, tell them or show them what that looks like, and be very clear about it. I am hoping that your school has a behaviour-management framework that includes steps for managing poor conduct and escalating your concerns if it persists. These steps might include restorative justice, a range of punitive consequences, a withdrawal room, parental meetings and so forth. Whatever it is, it starts with the teacher. If poor behaviour does persist, you're not alone and you shouldn't put up with it. When a student is affecting their own learning, the learning of others and your ability to teach, it's a problem that needs to be jumped on.

Give yourself a few minutes to wrap up at the end of the lesson by doing these three things:

1. Summarise what was learned
2. Check understanding with a couple of group or individual questions
3. Tell them what is coming up and what to prepare for, linking it to the broader unit

Finally, leave the classroom neat and tidy for the next teacher and class. It signals to the kids that the classroom is a place to be respected, and that we also respect the next teacher and class. Teaching is a collaborative exercise, and keeping the space that you share organised and clean for the next user is the right thing to do.

Classroom management checklist

Segment of lesson	Items to consider	Tick off as you go
Pre-lesson	Class list: names and numbers	
	Room layout, size, furniture available	
	Equipment needed	
	Illnesses, allergies, medical conditions	
	Student conduct or developmental issues	
	Seating plan best serving the type of lesson you wish to deliver	
	Technology needed (check that it works!)	
	How the students will enter the room	
	The first thing you want them to do when they enter the room	
	Whether there's a phone in the room or nearby	
	Lesson plan and content	
Start of lesson	Seating arrangements	
	How you'll get the attention of the class	
	Whether you'll have something already written on the board or shown on the data projector	
	Where you'll position yourself	
	Whether you'll need to distribute worksheets	
During the lesson	What to do if WiFi drops out	
	What to do if a student is off-task	
	Whether you plan to move around the room	
	What to do if a student finishes a task early	
	What to do if you need to move on but a few students have not finished	
	Where you'll move a student if needed (do you have a spare chair and will they remain within sight?)	

Segment of lesson	Items to consider	Tick off as you go
End of lesson	Whether you'll set homework	
	How you'll check for understanding	
	How the students will pack up	
	How you'll dismiss the class	
	Who puts the equipment away and whether there is a routine for this	
	How you'll exit the classroom	
Post-lesson	What the next lesson is and what needs to be done before then	
	What worked well and what didn't work well	
	Who you need to move	
	Whether you need to be more proactive	
	Whether you need more supplies or equipment	
	Whether you need a new or adjusted seating plan	

Three key points from this chapter

1. Classroom management is proactive, behaviour management is reactive
2. Classroom management starts with prior planning
3. Deal with poor behaviour and prevent it from derailing the class by having a strategy and shared expectations

12

Teacher performance and development

The greatest school impact on student achievement is the quality of the teacher (Jensen, Hunter, Sonnemann, & Cooper, 2014; OECD, 2011). It stands to reason that one of the main goals of school leaders should be to foster quality teachers. One of the most effective ways to do this is through a performance and development process also known as teacher evaluation or appraisal.

Fairly logical, right?

The problem here is that the development and implementation of such a process is difficult to achieve. Before I get into this, notice that I'm saying *teacher* quality and not *teaching* quality. Teacher quality covers the entire role of the teacher, not just what they do in the classroom. This is not an assessment of character. It describes how a person fares as a teacher and the qualities they bring to the school, the children, their colleagues, the school community and the profession. A teacher performance and development process should be about everything that you do inside and outside the classroom. A lot of your best work will occur outside.

A teacher performance and development process is not punitive. It is not about managing poor performance. This is a separate process that is done with a staff member who is underperforming and needs very clear and targeted intervention with specific timelines, clear outcomes and a support plan. This process might fall out of the performance and development process, but it is not the focus.

Sometimes the words evaluation and appraisal cause anxiety for a teacher. It's only natural to feel like this! We all get a bit nervous when we know we're being assessed, judged, scrutinised. Many schools don't use these terms for this reason. The inclusion of the word *development* indicates that growth and improvement are key parts of this process, or at least should be. As teachers we assess other people every day, so we need to be comfortable in being assessed ourselves. Despite the anxiety that might come with that, it is healthy to seek continual improvement. We role-model this to our students by letting them know that we want to improve and we want their feedback.

For a teacher performance and development process to be effective, some fundamental aspects need to be considered. Early-career teachers often simply inherit the process at their school, but it's important to understand what works and what doesn't.

The secrets of an effective performance and development process

There should be at least three pieces of data or evidence collected to inform the process. These may include peer observation, self-reflection, a student survey or a portfolio of evidence. This allows for triangulation of data and provides a breadth of information to start a conversation.

The process should go for an entire school year. It starts with setting some goals and a conversation, and it ends with a review and a conversation. A typical school year in Australia runs from late January to early December. The initial conversation should be done by the end of February. The final conversation should be done before the teacher leaves for their Christmas holiday break. It is cyclical: a teacher who returns year after year should simply carry on from the year prior and build on their goals, feedback and reflections. The process should be very collaborative, conversational and relational.

The person who is doing the evaluation must be someone you respect and trust. The success or failure of the process hinges on this one thing. There is simply no point in receiving feedback on your teaching ability from someone who cannot teach, or who treats the whole process as a burdensome administrative exercise.

If time is not intentionally set aside, it will not work. The process is human-intensive and teachers need to have rich conversations. The importance of these conversations to student outcomes and teacher fulfilment means that they should take priority on the calendar.

Feedback must be frequent, regular and timely. Do not leave it to the end of the year before a substantial conversation is held. The feedback must have depth and be constructive.

Red flags

Here are 10 red flags to watch out for as a teacher seeking opportunities to develop. If you find yourself in a school where these things are in place, know that the teacher performance and development process is weak. This means that you will have limited to no professional growth from the process. Beyond your own professional growth, it signals that there is little focus on teacher improvement. This means that there is little focus on student improvement. We have one job as educators, and that's student improvement. If we aren't working towards this goal then we may as well collect our toys and go home.

1. No process in place whatsoever: beware a school without a process where there is at least some reflection or feedback on performance, or even some mentoring
2. No start-of-year conversation with a line manager, and therefore no development plan put in place either at the start of the year or after a completed cycle
3. No time set aside for the process
4. Only one piece of evidence in the form of a self-assessment (honestly, who is really going to fail themselves!)
5. No benchmark, criteria or standards

6. No end-of-year conversation, wrap-up, feedback or reflections on performance
7. A mentor whom you do not trust or respect
8. The whole process being seen as a tick-a-box exercise
9. Poor performers continuing year after year with no interventions
10. A line manager who does not know how to interpret the data, or lacks the skill or experience to provide useful feedback

The role of school culture

The relationship between a teacher and the person responsible for their performance evaluation is important, but school culture surrounding the process helps significantly. School culture refers to explicit and implicit behaviours, language and engagement patterns that exist within a school. It is the climate of trust and relationships between teachers, students and parents. As an individual teacher, you may not have a great deal of influence on the perception and implementation of the performance and development process. There are, however, some very clear and relatively easy things that can have a massive impact.

School culture must invest in the following:

- **An emphasis on teacher improvement.** Focusing on improvement rather than accountability or administration is critical if teachers are to view the exercise as worthwhile. There are many things that the leadership team of a school can do to ensure this: they can allow time to conduct a worthwhile evaluation, collect a wide variety of evidence, acknowledge excellent performance, manage poor performance and devise personalised development plans post-evaluation.
- **Value placed on feedback.** It is the collective responsibility of all staff to promote a school culture that encourages feedback. Although the principal and management team play a significant role in leading and facilitating this mindset, it is the teaching staff who will embed, practice and normalise it in their daily actions. This feedback culture

must be framed in a way that is developmental, regular, in-depth, specific and drawn from a variety of evidence.

- **Regular dialogue around teacher quality and teaching quality.** This delivers two outcomes to a school. First, all teachers come to know the importance of teacher quality and their core business of quality teaching. Second, all teachers have a baseline understanding of the core features that are considered quality practices, skills, aptitudes and characteristics, and can implement these in their classroom pedagogy (see Chapter 6).
- **A common understanding of quality teaching shared by evaluator and teacher.** This is an extension of the previous recommendation. While regular dialogue around quality teaching is important, it must create a common understanding of the identified areas for improvement. This understanding leads to mutually-agreed goals and a development plan.
- **Knowledge of the Australian Professional Standards for Teachers (the Standards or APST), or the criteria or benchmarks used for evaluation.** The teacher must know what they will be judged against, what is expected of them and what best practice looks like across a variety of domains. This needs to be communicated to the teacher at the start of the evaluation cycle. Although the APST framework provides a sound set of criteria upon which to build a teacher evaluation tool, it is quite acceptable for a school to modify or add to these criteria.

Three key points from this chapter

1. The development process makes a huge difference to teacher and student success
2. The process is built on trust and relationships
3. Everyone in the school should share an understanding of what quality teaching looks like

13

Differentiation: how does it work?

As a teacher, you need to get your head around the concept of differentiation. It means delivering content in such a way that all kids in your class have a fighting chance of remembering it, understanding it, and doing something meaningful and worthwhile with it.

Here is my very own definition of differentiation: the ability to reach and engage with all students in your class regardless of their ability, intelligence or background.

Differentiation means tailoring your teaching and assessment to account for the varying needs and abilities of the students in your class. By strategically aligning your planning with individual learners, you will help them to not only meet standards but to potentially excel.

This all sounds very heart-warming, doesn't it? Except that it is impossible to do for every child. Any school that claims they truly personalise learning is kidding themselves. Unless that school has very small class sizes and a generous student-to-teacher ratio, personalised learning won't occur. For a typical mainstream school rolling out the Australian Curriculum across multiple classes and subjects, a degree of differentiation is certainly expected. But it won't be personalised for every child in every subject and every lesson by every teacher. When I was a PE specialist, some years I didn't even know all the kids' names until the end of Term 1. I had 5 classes with between 25 to 30 kids per class, and on some occasions only one lesson per week with each class. So my ability to personalise for every child clearly wasn't enabled.

Personalisation might occur in some primary schools where students are mostly taught by one teacher, especially when class sizes are small. Secondary school teachers, on the other hand, might teach up to 125 students per term. Each of these students will have 5 teachers and they too will each have 125 students of their own. Will these teachers all have a personalised plan for each child? I don't think so. Not if they want to make it to Easter upright and breathing.

Differentiation isn't just about taking the core content and somehow making it a bit easier for the kids who are at the learning-support end of the spectrum, or a bit harder for the smarter cookies in the class. It also isn't about just giving kids more or less work to do based on their ability level. Before the purists gasp with disdain, let's not get too fancy: both approaches may be a valid way to differentiate the curriculum for your class, and I've employed them plenty of times with great success. Sometimes the basic stuff works just fine, and sometimes that's all we have time for. There are a few models floating around that provide some very good ways to differentiate learning. The Maker model (1982) suggests four ways to differentiate curriculum through modifications to the learning environment, the content, the process and the product. Carol Ann Tomlinson (*The Differentiated Classroom: Responding to the Needs of All Learners*, 1995) is a prolific writer and researcher on differentiation in the classroom, as close as a guru as you can get. She takes the aforementioned ways to differentiate a step further by suggesting that we also consider a student's readiness, interests and learning profile (their learning styles and preferences).

I like to keep things even simpler, so I tend to differentiate my curriculum along the complexity of content, the assessment and the instructional methods.

Differentiating my curriculum

Complexity of content	Assessment	Instructional methods
There is core content that needs to be covered. This can be adapted to become more or less complex for the different learners in the class.	The ways in which kids show their mastery of the content can be modified.	Some children prefer collaboration, some prefer quiet individual study. Know the learning styles of your kids and choose methods that resonate accordingly.

You now have a grasp of what differentiation is, and how to differentiate your content and curriculum. Great. The final piece of the puzzle is to apply this across a class of students. When you do your planning, you'll soon ascertain which students need support and which need extension. You'll do this via pre-assessment tools, the assessment tasks themselves, diagnostic tests and so forth. Once these things are determined, you can plan for them. Personalisation for each child may not be feasible, but you can plan for segments, bands or groups of children.

The Triple C differentiation model

I don't know if there is an actual term for the differentiation method that I use, but I call it the three-part or Triple C model: Consolidation—Core—Complexity.

Core is the mandated curriculum that every child should have an opportunity to access. Consolidation is the way in which I modify the core to simplify it or make it more accessible. Complexity is the way in which I modify the core to make it more challenging or expansive. In Chapter 2, I shared two lesson plans with differentiation samples built in. I'll now tease out these lesson plans to show you how to implement the Triple C model.

Year 2: Thinking About Time

Consolidation	Core	Complexity
Focus on big hand and little hand. Big hand is minute hand, little hand is hour hand. Provide simple scenarios. Focus on 3 o'clock, 6 o'clock, 9 o'clock and 12 o'clock on printable sheets.	As per lesson plan. 1 o'clock through to 12 o'clock. Tell time to the hour. Use printable sheets. Basic terms. Provide a range of scenarios.	Provide them with more complex scenarios to solve. Or give them a scenario with a half-hour inclusion.

Year 8: Health, Nutrition and Food Groups

Consolidation	Core	Complexity
Focus on the 5 and 6 rule. Write these on a simple graphic organiser and provide 1 example for each. Yunus and James will need additional support.	As per lesson plan. Complete the task sheets as per instructions.	Students can explore additional vitamins and minerals and their purpose. For example: Vitamin B12 comes from sardines and helps produce red blood cells. Check on Emma and her progress.

Three key points from this chapter

1. It's unrealistic to personalise for every child, so differentiation is your ally
2. Differentiate your content, assessment and instructional methods
3. Core—Consolidation—Complexity: these segments will help you cater for all learners

14

Future skills: what else do we need to teach and how do we do it?

The need to teach skills that kids might need for the future is covered ad nauseum in newspapers, books, articles, blogs, podcasts, TV shows and conference discussions. These skills are usually called 21st-century skills, 21st-century learning or future skills.

However they are branded, the skills will usually include creativity, communication, problem-solving, resilience, digital literacy and collaboration. Other skills may be entrepreneurship, critical thinking, global awareness and environmental awareness.

One thing everyone always says after rattling off these skills is that schools are responsible for embedding them. Before we know it, the same commentators will get all hot and bothered about another social failure or catastrophe. Guess what? This too must now be dealt with by schools.

So while teachers are rolling out yet another version of the Australian Curriculum, providing senior schooling pathways for all learners, tackling social and emotional wellbeing, trying to differentiate, managing the poor behaviour of disenchanted teenagers and undertaking child protection training, what else are we doing? We're working out how to embed creativity and entrepreneurial skills. We're covering topics such as consent education, safe driver training, responsible alcohol consumption, responsible masculinity and respectful relationships to name but a few. And Australians wonder why our nation continues to struggle with the fundamentals of literacy and numeracy, and why teaching has such a high attrition rate.

I don't disagree with the need to cover these skills. It's a noble pursuit, but we must consider the practicalities of allocating time for new content in an already-crowded school day. Ask any parent what they want for their child at primary school. Most will want their child to be safe, to know the basics of literacy and numeracy, to achieve at least satisfactorily and to get along with others. This continues at secondary school, except that parents also want their child to be emotionally stable and find a suitable career pathway.

So what do things like problem-solving, entrepreneurship and resilience actually look like, and how do we embed them within a curriculum? We already encounter plenty of kids putting all their effort into simply being able to sit still for extended periods of time. Add in a nebulous topic like resilience and I say good luck to you sir. The key to covering these topics is to not do them in isolation. *Hi kids, welcome to Lesson 6. Today we are going to cover a topic called resilience. Who can give me an example of resilience?* I can almost hear the groans now! The worst thing that we can do is to give kids a lecture about resilience, digital responsibility, environmental awareness and so forth. These topics must be part of something worthwhile, practical, interesting and fun. It's up to us educators to make this happen. These topics need to be embedded across a variety of school activities and subject areas. It's not the sole responsibility of a single department or subject area, or of those tasked with pastoral care. In the same way that it's not just up to English teachers to teach literacy, entrepreneurial skills shouldn't only be taught in Business.

We have a responsibility as educators to look at creative ways of modifying and adapting our curriculum, school day and school year to expose our kids to these skills. We need to model entrepreneurial skills, critical thinking, collaboration and problem-solving to make it work.

Ways to model new skills we wish to embed

- Projects and assessment tasks that require collaboration
- Service learning programs that involve community engagement with those less fortunate, and opportunities for students to give something of themselves
- Entrepreneurial opportunities that include innovative ways to solve a problem, to make a profit, to serve the community (these can double as an assessment task)
- Coping with adversity using compassion, strength, empathy and patience
- Helping our children deal with loss or failure without giving up, getting depressed, becoming afraid to give it a go
- Showing the courage to take educated risks and having the fortitude to bounce back when things don't work
- Fostering student mentoring opportunities across year levels
- Creating leadership opportunities, and not just for those who wear the badge or shine at public speaking: student leadership comes in all guises, so sniff it out and build it up
- A variety of after-school, before-school and in-school activities that provide options for students of all abilities, year levels and interests
- School camps. Look, I get it! It's not every teacher's idea of fun to sleep in a tent on a thin bit of foam, surrounded in minimal privacy by teenagers with dubious body odour. But the things I have seen kids do at camp are simply brilliant and cannot be replicated at school. The kids grow and learn about themselves and others, often very quickly.

It's through these experiences that kids learn resilience, teamwork, problem-solving, creativity and so forth. Pitching a tent in the rain after hiking all day and then having to cook a meal—as uncomfortable as that sounds—will teach a kid more than they will ever learn about resilience in front of a PowerPoint or a guest speaker.

Finally, at risk of adding more to the list of things that ought to be squeezed into a school week, and completely going against my views on this topic,

I'd like to suggest the following elements to incorporate into our planning for the school year.

Learning with real-life application

- **Human skills.** Be kind, be thoughtful, be considerate. It doesn't cost anything. We focus on character traits like humility, empathy and gratitude. Kindness trumps them all.
- **Combating loneliness.** This will be one of our biggest future social burdens. We've never been more connected globally, yet we are disconnected locally. So learn how to make friends and sustain friendships, and how to reach out to those who may be lonely.
- **Personal finance and money management.** Learning these basics will reduce so much pain and suffering later in life. There are so many things we are magically expected to know: how to manage a personal and family budget, how to obtain various insurances, how to get a bank loan, how to buy a house, how to rent, how we're affected by interest rates, how to balance cost-of-living pressures.
- **Media literacy.** Accessing information is not the problem. Filtering information and deciding what is worth taking notice of or ignoring is the challenge.
- **Practical life skills.** Cooking a meal, changing a car tyre, maintaining a home, ironing a shirt, the etiquette expected at various events.
- **Work ethic.** Grinding out a day's work, then a week's, then a year's. Doing so even when exhausted! Being prompt, dressing appropriately for a role, taking pride in the quality of our work.
- **Service skills.** Doing something for others and expecting nothing in return. Doing something simply to make someone's life a bit easier. Doing something for others to enrich our communities.

Three key points from this chapter

1. We need to be creative and clever by including new skills in projects, activities and experiences (think hiding veggies in pasta sauce to make sure our kids eat their greens!)

2. As important as things like entrepreneurship and collaboration are, don't lose sight of the attributes that give us our humanity: kindness, friendship, empathy and service

3. Wake up, get up, lace up, turn up: if kids do these things every day, most other things take care of themselves

15

Collegiality: we all need a teacher buddy

If one more non-teacher person tries to tell me that:

- I must have become a teacher to get school holidays
- I get school holidays so I should consider myself fortunate
- I really only work from 9am to 3pm
- They themselves are considering becoming a teacher because of the holidays

I will come seriously close to being on the nightly news for all the wrong reasons.

I can just see the headlines now:

> *Middle-aged teacher attempts to strangle man at neighbourhood BBQ after being told that he only became a teacher for the holidays.*

Or

> *Large fat hairy man who calls himself a principal has mental breakdown in local shopping centre after bumping into parent who suggested he must enjoy all that time off and noted that he himself might retrain as a teacher to enjoy same. Police left dumbfounded by this apparent overreaction.*

For anyone interested, I'll let you in on a few secrets.

Teachers don't become teachers for the holidays. Someone doesn't decide to dedicate their life to this profession just so they can have extra days off and then be miserable every other day.

What some may call holidays aren't in fact holidays at all. These are the days when we:

- Mark
- Report
- Attend professional development training
- Upskill ourselves
- Meet to complete a project
- Conduct research
- Work on our classrooms
- Create worksheets, task sheets, activities and games
- Clean up art rooms, sport sheds, tech labs and science labs
- Purchase and re-stock for the term or year ahead
- Coach sporting teams
- Run training or student leadership camps
- Plan and design lessons, units and assessments
- Create wonderful digital technology units with myriad links, clips and multimedia

This is commonly called work. If you're thinking about becoming a teacher for the holidays—and by holidays you mean 10 to 12 weeks per year—do us all a favour and find another career. If you are a teacher who takes every holiday 'off' and complain that you don't get enough time to plan, the same advice applies. School holidays aren't teacher holidays. Don't get the two confused. They are holidays for the kids, but they allow us to deal with the teaching tasks that aren't forward-facing.

Teaching can be physically and mentally demanding. You're 'on' all the time. You're the actor on a stage performing multiple shows a day. You will be dealing with students of various ages, interests, abilities and backgrounds. Some students will have learning difficulties. Some will have behavioural and conduct issues that will test your sanity. Some will be self-harming due to a mental illness, past trauma or even current trauma. Some will be withdrawn, and others will want your attention constantly. Some will confide in you because you may be the only adult whom they trust. Some will be anxious, depressed, have OCD, ADHD, oppositional defiant disorder (ODD) or autism. Some will be slow learners and others will be fast learners, while plenty will be in the middle. You'll need to cater for all of them. And all of this will flash before your eyes before lunchtime on a Monday. Then of course there is the planning, the marking, the admin, the parental contact and plenty of meetings. If anyone out there thinks they can easily do this teaching thing, then I offer them the keys to the classroom. I'll even throw in a few whiteboard markers. And remember, the kids will sense your fear. Good luck.

I'm not painting a very bright picture here. But teaching happens to be the most rewarding career I could ever imagine. If you want to thrive, you'll need some mates in the trenches with you. Teaching is not something you do alone. If that's the model that you have in mind, it's wrong. The best model is one of collegiality, sharing and openness.

Why?

You'll need to vent to a colleague who understands. Sure, we all have other people to talk to. But if they aren't teachers, aides or serving in another kind of teaching role then they won't understand.

You'll want to share ideas, strategies, tips and tools around a unit of work, an activity, a task or even a student. You'll benefit from someone else looking over your assessment tasks and your marking. You'll need help with an excursion, an incursion, a camp, a carnival, an event, a dance, a formal, a parent night or a fete.

Above all, you'll need to enjoy coming to work every day. It's the people you work with who make the difference. The people who share your sense of humour, who pick you up when you are down and share in your birthdays, births, deaths, illnesses, divorces, graduations. You need a few mates to help you weather the teaching game.

Toxic staffrooms (and people)

Toxic staff can derail an entire school. Interesting tensions and dynamics arise when a group of people from various backgrounds come together in a small space for extended periods of time, sometimes under extreme pressure and often seeing each other more than they do their own families. Usually in a toxic staffroom there is a dominant personality who garners support from a couple of likeminded but timid colleagues who view the world through a negative lens. People like this come together at regular intervals to tell each other how great they are and how hard they all work, exclaiming that no one else knows anything. Like the Sith Lords in *Star Wars* they get their strength from negativity, sucking the light and joy out of the room. These little groups are negative about everything: students, management, new initiatives, life in general. New initiatives are their speciality. If these initiatives are not their idea or threaten their little power base, they'll shoot them down with some skill. They will undermine, snipe and vocalise their concerns. If others try to be positive, they'll shoot those people down as well. Eventually others won't say anything at all, and the grumpy group run their own narrative. A staffroom won't become toxic when there's only one negative nelly; this person can be sidelined quickly by positive souls and will either shut up or leave. If a negative group gets hold of the room, then it's the good people who will leave.

So what do we do about it? This is one of the hardest things I've had to deal with as a principal. It's hard to take a stand as a teacher if you want to see change. You might have the courage to say something, but I've not seen this very often. Toxic people need to be confronted by someone in a leadership role. The inmates can't be left to run the asylum.

Confronting toxicity

If you are in a leadership role and have the unenviable job of tackling a staff member's toxic attitude, here are a few tips.

Always start with a private conversation. Ask the person you're concerned about if everything is okay. Mention that you can see that they are disgruntled or anxious about something. Say that you've noticed this having a negative impact on the staffroom, their colleagues, your ability to roll out certain things. Give them an opportunity to talk, respond and improve. Write down some notes on the conversation. Try to forge a positive path forward. I always follow up with a summary email that lists the concerns, what was spoken about and steps forward. If the toxicity continues, the next conversation will have to be more direct with clearly outlined expectations. If these aren't met, a formal performance-management process will need to be implemented.

One of three things will happen: they'll change their actions, they'll leave in a disgruntled huff and puff or they'll dig in. The first scenario is unlikely. The second is preferred. If the staff member digs in, the response of the school will set the tone and culture for years to come. As teachers we don't get much training on this sort of stuff when we step into a leadership role. These interventions are probably the most uncomfortable and challenging thing you'll have to do in the workplace. But if you wear the badge and collect the extra coin, then saddle up and get to it. You'll feel better for it, you'll keep good staff, and most importantly you'll get to roll out initiatives that have an impact on those who matter: the students.

Three key points from this chapter

1. Don't become a teacher for the holidays
2. The best culture model is one of collegiality, sharing and openness
3. Toxic staffrooms and employees need to be addressed as soon as possible

16
A brief blurb about AITSL and the Australian Professional Standards for Teachers

The Australian Institute for Teaching and School Leadership (AITSL) was formed in 2010 to develop the Australian Professional Standards for Teachers (the Standards or APST) in consultation with teachers throughout Australia. The completion of the process in 2011 established Australia's first clear and nationally accepted articulation of what teachers were expected to know and do across all states and territories. This was followed by the publication of the *Australian Teacher Performance and Development Framework* (AITSL, 2012), which provides a platform to implement the Standards as part of teacher improvement processes within schools. The premise underpinning *The Standards* is that the quality of teachers is the most important in-school element affecting student outcomes (AITSL, 2012; Barber & Mourshed, 2007; Hattie, 2012; OECD, 2009).

The Standards incorporate three teaching domains (Professional Knowledge, Professional Practice and Professional Engagement) across four career stages of teaching (Graduate, Proficient, Highly Accomplished and Lead). Professional Knowledge refers to teachers' knowledge of their subjects and students, and to their application of developmentally appropriate teaching and learning strategies. Professional Practice refers to teachers' ability to create and maintain safe, inclusive and challenging learning environments. Professional Engagement refers to teachers' ability to expand their own professional learning and to engage with their wider school community.

The table below sets out the Standards, aligning each against one of the three Domains of Teaching representing the scope and role of the teacher and the teaching profession (AITSL, 2011).

The Australian Professional Standards for Teachers

Domain of Teaching	Standards
Professional Knowledge	Know students and how they learn
	Know the content and how to teach it
Professional Practice	Plan for and implement effective teaching and learning
	Create and maintain supportive and safe environments
	Assess, provide feedback and report on student learning
Professional Engagement	Engage in professional learning
	Engage professionally with colleagues, parents/carers and the community

A teacher's progression through the four career stages demonstrates a growing understanding and application of pedagogy across a range of situations. Graduate teachers meet the requirements of a nationally accredited program of beginner teacher education. Proficient teachers develop and implement engaging learning programs that fulfil curriculum, assessment and reporting obligations. Highly Accomplished teachers are effective and skilled classroom practitioners. Lead teachers are recognised and respected by colleagues, parents and their community as exemplary teachers.

You'll need to provide evidence of your competency in the Standards to attain registration as a teacher in Australia. Most (if not all) Australian universities will use the Standards in their teacher training programs.

The Standards provide a platform for schools to establish a collective understanding of what effective teaching looks like. As such, schools have increasingly used the Standards as a mechanism to conduct their own methods of teacher appraisal.

Three key points from this chapter

1. The Standards tell teachers what they are expected to know and do
2. There are seven Standards, three Domains of Teaching and four career phases
3. Schools are encouraged to refer to the Standards in their teacher appraisal processes

17

Getting yourself classroom-fit

We teachers need to sustain our energy and wellbeing day after day, week after week and term after term for the entire school year. Teaching is a customer-facing job. You are the leader, the conductor, the trainer, the sage on stage, the guide by the side. This is physically and emotionally demanding, and if you don't get yourself classroom-fit you will burn out.

You can't hide away behind a laptop or in an office cubicle. You can't have long lunches or pop out of the office for a massage. You can't have a quiet day, a lazy afternoon or a cruisy Monday after a big weekend. You must bring your best self every day. If you don't, the kids will make it a living hell for you. Sure, we all have days where we are tired or grappling with illness, tragic news or family complications. We need to develop a few coping mechanisms so that when these things occur we can get ourselves back on track with as little difficulty as possible.

So what can you do?

Develop a baseline of physical fitness. Teaching is an active job. It's not digging holes, building fences or laying tiles. But you will be moving around a campus and a classroom. You will be on playground duty. You will be constantly using your voice and body to communicate. You will be talking to a variety of people. You will be carrying textbooks, laptops and resources. You will be going to meetings, planning lessons and marking assessment. You might be coaching a sporting team, have an event to attend in the evening or even a weekend school commitment or a camp. On most days you'll get approximately 10 to 15 minutes of lunchtime to yourself. This occurs daily for at least 40 weeks of the year, and those other weeks are set aside for professional development, planning, research, stocktaking and so forth.

This means you have to look after yourself physically with exercise that includes both cardio and weight training. It will sustain you, give you strength and make you feel better about yourself. Having a decent level of physical fitness means you won't fall asleep on the couch exhausted every night at 7.30pm. It means you won't hit that wall in Week 8 of a 10-week term. It means you'll still be strong in Lesson 6 on a Friday afternoon, when you find yourself in front of 25 Year 9 kids who want that lesson to go quicker than you do.

So how much physical fitness do you need? Here is a rule of thumb: can you do a single push-up? I don't mean on your knees, or with your bum sticking up in the air. I mean a full push-up. Can you walk up a single flight of stairs without puffing, feeling a burning sensation in your quads or needing to stop at the top to catch your breath? If you said no to one or both of these then you have a bit of work to do. Walking, running, aerobics, weightlifting, Pilates, swimming, tennis, touch football, soccer, it all counts. Get some exercise at least a few times per week. Please note that the following pursuits do not classify as exercise for the purposes of the teaching profession: lawn bowls, darts, gardening, archery, shopping or pub crawls.

You also have to switch off. Teachers take stuff home all the time. Sometimes it's unavoidable, especially around heavy marking and reporting periods. But if you don't find a way to switch off, the classroom will remain in your head every waking minute. Sometimes it will creep into your dreams. You'll wake up exhausted. So what can you do? Find something that fills your bucket. I'm not here to talk about anything too deep and complicated, and you won't find yourself in the lotus position humming something unintelligible with me.

How to switch off

Here are some things that I find helpful, and that I know have worked for others.

- **Friends and family.** Not a great surprise, I know. But I'd like to suggest something apart from the obvious benefit of emotional support. It's simply important to have people to spend time and have fun with so that work does not become your only point of social contact. You need the opportunity to do things apart from lesson planning and teaching! Friends and family give you purpose outside of work, and you can plan enjoyable things to do together that will sustain you when you are mid-term. They give you something to look forward to.

- **Hobbies and other interests.** Again, apart from the obvious need to do things that feed your soul, I'll share something else that gives me some sanity. Every school holiday I'll put some time aside to do house renovations. Nothing huge, as I don't have great handyman skills or even great workmanship. Generally it's painting: walls, fences, ceilings, carports, even floors. If it's flat and stays still long enough, it gets painted. I don't need to think too much, I don't need to talk too much, I don't have too many decisions to make, it's a little bit physical and active, and I can have the cricket on the radio playing in the background. Wonderful stuff.

   I recently read about something called an 'opposite world'. It's the thing that a person does in their free time that is completely different to their work. For instance, my friend is an accountant. It pays the bills but he finds it mind-numbing. His true passion is marathon running. He travels all over the country going on running staycations.

- **Alone time.** A teacher will interact with people all day, make thousands of decisions and respond to thousands of questions. It can be draining. You need to recharge, and you'll benefit from some time alone to do so. That might mean reading a book, going on a hike, hitting the gym, doing some renovation work, going on a road trip, binging on the latest TV series. Whatever it is for you, try to find some of it.

Cut a few corners

Now that we've covered what we should be doing in our downtime, here are some little tips to help you throughout the year when you're at school.

- **Here's one I prepared earlier.** Have a bunch of tasks, worksheets and activities ready to go for your classes and subject area. These are your time-fillers, your crutch, your saviours.
- **Get tech sorted.** If you have an LMS (Learning Management System), upload videos and links ahead of time so they'll be ready to go when needed.
- **Don't be a loner.** Build your networks at school, you'll need them.
- **Think outside the ordinary teaching box.** This will build the capacity of your kids. Routines are wonderful. So are extra resources at the ready in your room.
- **Get your classroom set up the way you need and want it.** You might be sharing classrooms with other teachers, so collaborate with them on desk positioning to save time and reduce anxiety.
- **Use your wall space.** Put up class rules, academic reminders and prompts for the kids so they won't pester you when they finish a task. Displaying the class rules on the wall means that you can draw attention to them as a simple behaviour-management strategy when needed.
- **Get some time-fillers.** Have board games, simple art tasks and brain teasers ready to go. Do not revert to screening a movie via your preferred streaming service.
- **Prior planning prevents poor performance.** No, you aren't about to read Chapter 2 all over again, but plan you must in order to preserve your sanity. Plan for when you may need it the most, because tough moments will come for you at some point in the year. The more front-ending you can do, the greater your ability to weather the storms of school and your own personal life.

Three key points from this chapter

1. Teaching is not a sedentary job: you need a baseline of fitness to survive and thrive
2. It's okay to cut a few corners, just remember to plan
3. Find some ways to fill your buckets outside school

Conclusion

If you've made it this far in the book, I'd like to congratulate you. Either you've read it cover-to-cover or you've gone straight to the last chapter to decide whether it's worth your time to read the whole damn thing. Don't worry, we've all done it. You're clearly interested enough to delve a bit deeper, you care enough to be a bit better, and you're curious enough to learn a bit more about the mysteries of the classroom and the work of a teacher.

Our world and our profession are changing rapidly. Teaching and classrooms didn't superficially change a great deal between the 1800s and the early 1990s. Take a look at an old grainy black-and-white photo and compare it to a photo of a classroom in the late 20th century. I can almost guarantee that the kids will be sitting in rows in a four-wall classroom looking at a teacher at the front.

If you were to walk into one of my classrooms today, you'd see a similar picture at times. Desks, chairs, rows, all eyes looking to me as I dish out content in a fairly rigid and conventional manner. But don't be deceived; our profession has changed a lot in recent years. COVID, as hellish as it was, accelerated this change. It is important for schools and teachers to get ahead of change and harness it for positive learning purposes. Education is in an extremely exciting period, with new technologies enabling us to transform how we teach, learn and 'do' schooling. We also have great responsibilities and challenges, which we must meet with the same qualities we are trying to instil in our kids: courage, resilience, creativity, communication, problem-solving and collaboration. We must teach children how to be responsible with technology and identify digital garbage to protect themselves and others.

Technology has opened many doors, but it has also created a new set of challenges for teachers and schools. Its influence has changed the way some kids and parents view the institution of school and has lessened their respect for teachers. It has changed how they interact with their world, how they respond to hardship and adversity, how they cope with mental health challenges. Media and information platforms affect our time, trust, decisions and relationships. The teacher-parent relationship is affected by changes in workplaces and family structures and by higher rates of movement across schools, states and countries.

As other professions become more automated, the role of the teacher has never been more important. Human interaction sparks the magic of learning, social interactions at school prepare kids for life, and many school staff care for their students just as parents do. In an increasingly busy, hostile, complex and disconnected world, school and teacher are the bedrock for children and often for their families. Schools are the new churches and community hubs. They are places of social connection and friendship for many people.

You'll notice that both the introduction and the conclusion of this book focus on the human condition. This is because the work of the teacher is first and foremost about relationships. It's a 'heart' job, a profession to which we become deeply connected. We are in the business of building a little human every day, every year, sometimes for several years. We help them build their character, their skills, their confidence, their resilience. We help them understand themselves, others and their world. We take them virtually as toddlers, and we see them off as adults. I think it is one of the most important jobs in the world. We don't teach content, we teach people. We teach them to take their place in society as well-adjusted, contributing and thoughtful individuals. Welcome to the teaching game. It is, in fact, the game of life.

References

AllPlay Learn. (2022, September 8). *Home – AllPlay Learn.* https://allplaylearn.org.au/

Aspect Australia | Autism Spectrum Australia (Aspect). (n.d.). Autism Spectrum Australia (Aspect). https://www.autismspectrum.org.au/

Attwood, T. (2009). *The Complete Guide to Aspergers Syndrome.* London. Jessica Kingsley Publishers.

Australian Institute for Teaching and School Leadership (AITSL). (2011). *Australian Professional Standards for Teachers.* Canberra: Australian Government.

Australian Institute for Teaching and School Leadership (AITSL). (2012). *Australian Teacher and Performance Development Framework.* Canberra: Australian Government.

Barber, M., & Mourshed, M. (2007). *How the world's best performing school systems come out on top.* London: McKinsey and Company.

Beardon, L. (2019). *Autism & Aspergers Syndrome in Children.* Sheldon Press. London.

Bloom, B. S. (1984). *Taxonomy of Educational Objectives* (2nd Ed.). Addison-Wesley Longman. New York.

Boulton-Lewis, G. M. (1995). The SOLO Taxonomy as a Means of Shaping and Assessing Learning in Higher Education. *Higher Education Research and Development,* 14(2), 143–154. https://doi.org/10.1080/0729436950140201

Britannica Concise Encyclopedia. (2006). Ukraine: Encyclopaedia Britannica.

Brizendine, L. (2011). *The Male Brain: A breakthrough understanding of how men and boys think.* Random House. New York.

Cambridge Advanced Learner's Dictionary. (2013). Brazil: Cambridge University Press.

de Bono, E. (2016). *Six Thinking Hats.* Penguin Books Limited.

Diagnostic and Statistical Manual of Mental Disorders (2022) American Psychiatric Association Publishing, Washington, DC. (5th Ed.)

Fisher, D. & Frey, N. (2021). *Better Learning Through Structured Teacher: A Framework for the Gradual Release of Responsibility Model.* New York: ASCD.

Fisk, S. (2022) *Using and Analysing Data in Australian Schools* (2nd Ed.). Melbourne. Hawker Brownlow.

Fuller, A. (2014) *Tricky Teens: How to create a great relationship with your teen – without going crazy.* Sydney. Finch Publishing.

Gardner, H. E. (1983). *Frames of Mind: the theory of multiple intelligences.* New York. Basic Books.

Gardner, H. E. (1993). *Multiple Intelligences: The Theory In Practice, A Reader.* Basic Books.

Genlott, A. A., Grönlund, Å., Viberg, O. & Andersson, A. (2021). Leading dissemination of digital, science-based innovation in school – a case study. *Interactive Learning Environments*, 1–11. https://doi.org/10.1080/10494820.2021.1955272

Gloria, R. Y., Sudarmin, Wiyanto & Indriyanti, D. R. (2018). Costa-Kallick's Habits of Mind in Practical Activities of Students as Teachers Candidate. *Edusains*, 10(1). https://doi.org/10.15408/es.v10i1.7208

Gurian, M. & Stevens, K. (2007). *The Minds of Boys: Saving our sons from falling behind in school and life.* Jossey-Bass. New York.

Hamilton, M. (2009) *What's happening to our girls?* Sydney. Penguin Group.

Hattie, J. (2012). *Visible Learning for Teachers.* New York: Routledge.

Healthy Eating. (2020, November 30). *Exploring the Five Food Groups* [Video]. YouTube. https://www.youtube.com/watch?v=KB-BomApiNo

Hewitson, J. (2018). *Autism: How to raise a happy autistic child.* Orion Spring. London.

Interpreting literacy assessment data. (n.d.). Education. https://www.education.vic.gov.au/school/teachers/learningneeds/Pages/interpreting-assessment-data-literacy.aspx/

Interpreting literacy assessment data. (n.d.-b). Victorian Department of Education. https://www.education.vic.gov.au/school/teachers/learningneeds/Pages/interpreting-assessment-data-literacy.aspx

Jensen, B., Hunter, J., Sonnemann, J., & Cooper, C. (2014). *Making time for great teaching.* Melbourne: Grattan Institute.

Jensen, F. E. (2015). *The Teenage Brain.* New York. Harper.

KIndlon, D. & Thompson, M. (2000). *Raising Cain: Protecting the emotional life of boys.* Random House Publishing Group. New York.

Larkey, S. (2005). *Making it a success: practical strategies and worksheets for teaching students with autism spectrum disorder.* Jessica Kingsley Publishers. London.

Lingard, B., Hayes, D., & Mills, M. (2003). Teachers and productive pedagogies: contextualising, conceptualising, utilising. *Pedagogy, Culture and Society*, 11(3), 399–424. https://doi.org/10.1080/14681360300200181

Maker, J. C. (1982). *Teaching models in education of the gifted.* Aspen Systems Corp. Rockville, MD.

Marzano, R. J. (2007). *The Art and Science of Teaching.* ASCD. Alexandria, VA.

Marzano, R.J. & Pickering, D. (1997). *Dimensions of Learning: Teacher's Manual.* ASCD. Alexandria, VA.

Mishra, P. & Koehler, M. J. (2006). Technological Pedagogical Content Knowledge: A Framework for Teacher Knowledge. *Teachers College Record*, 108(6), 1017–1054. https://doi.org/10.1111/j.1467-9620.2006.00684.x

NetflexKids.com: Studio. (2023, January 31). *Food Group Superheroes: Make-A-Plate THIS or THAT (Balanced Diet Activity)* [Video]. YouTube. https://www.youtube.com/watch?v=XFJU4ipwVVo

Norfleet-James, A. (2011). *Teaching the Female Brain.* Corwin Press. Thousand Oaks, USA.

OECD. (2009). *Creating effective teaching and learning environments: First results from TALIS.* Paris: OECD.

OECD. (2011). *Improving teacher quality around the world: The International summit on the teaching profession.* Paper presented at the Paper prepared for the International Summit on the teaching profession, New York. 15-16 March.

Price, D. (2022). *Unmasking Autism.* Octopus Publishing Group. London

Ritchhart, R. (2015). *Creating Cultures of Thinking: The 8 Forces We Must Master to Truly Transform Our Schools.* John Wiley & Sons.

School assessments. (n.d.). Australian Council for Educational Research – ACER. https://www.acer.org/au/assessment/school-assessments/

The Merriam-Webster Dictionary. (2022). United States: Merriam-Webster, Incorporated.

The Oxford English Dictionary. (1989). United Kingdom: Clarendon Press.

Tomlinson, C. A. (1995). The Differentiated Classroom: responding to the needs of all learners. (2nd Ed.). ASCD, Alexandria VA USA.

William, D. (2017). *Embedded formative assessment: strategies for classroom assessment that drives student engagement and learning.* (2nd ed.) Solution Tree Press: Bloomington. USA.

Acknowledgements

In writing this book I would like to acknowledge the contributions, feedback and suggestions of the following people:

Tamara Dunstan. Early-career teacher Tamara provided invaluable reflections on her university preparation, her teacher practicums and her first year in the classroom.

Peter Foster. A trusted colleague and an experienced principal who helped me distil what is most important for those doing the good work in classrooms every day.

Jason Day. I'd struggle to find a more diligent, hardworking, honest and committed educator. Jason's experience and his advice on this book were (as always) invaluable. He's the go-to person for most of my education questions.

Ronwyn Collier. I find it hard to sum up my admiration and respect for Ronwyn in a few words. I still can't believe the emotional investment that she puts into her school community, staff, students and parents every day. An inspiration.

All my colleagues throughout my career. What a blessing it has been to work with you all, to learn together, to struggle together, to achieve together. Thank you for joining me on the ride.

About the author

Damien is a career educator. Some would say he is somewhat institutionalised, as he went from high school to university then back to high school and never left! He'd have it no other way.

Starting in the mid-1990s, his career has spanned almost 30 years. Now a principal, Damien has worked in a variety of schools: primary, secondary, public, independent, all-girls, all-boys and co-ed. He's always been a classroom teacher and remains one to this day. He's been a deputy headmaster and college principal, has coordinated year levels, led schools and departments and headed campuses spanning two states.

Damien has an MBA and a Doctorate in Education. His thesis investigated best practices in teacher appraisal mechanisms. Being awarded a Churchill Fellowship afforded him the opportunity to travel the world to research and create rite-of-passage programs for teenage boys to reduce incidences of domestic violence. Damien aims to one day finish his career where it all started: in the classroom.

www.ingramcontent.com/pod-product-compliance
Lightning Source LLC
Chambersburg PA
CBHW050240120526
44590CB00016B/2167